Maggie Colvin's
HOME STYLE

Maggie Colvin's
HOME STYLE
Quick make-overs to transform your home

David & Charles

A DAVID & CHARLES BOOK

First published in the UK in 2001

A catalogue record for this book is available from the British Library.

ISBN 0 7153 1087 9

Commissioning editor   Lindsay Porter
Design and art direction   Ali Myer
Desk editor   Jennifer Proverbs
Text editor   Beverley Jollands
Photography   Jon Bouchier

Printed and bound in Italy by STIGE
for David & Charles
Brunel House   Newton Abbot   Devon

The author has made every effort to ensure that all the instructions in this book
are accurate and safe, and therefore cannot accept liability for any resulting injury,
damage or loss to persons or property however it may arise.

Contents

Introduction

The history of decoration is all about shifts in style, which come and go and often turn full circle. In today's global village the influences are wide and more readily accessible than ever before. Travelling abroad frequently, as many of us do, can be a dangerously inspirational business. If you are susceptible to pretty things, you may – like me – be tempted to buy, say, a Provençal tablecloth in a French market, and end up redecorating the entire kitchen to match it when you get home. One stylish souvenir can not only act as a permanent and precious reminder of a much-loved trip, but could lead you to create a whole new look.

It would be foolish not to look to other countries and past eras for inspiration. There is such a wealth to choose from. In an age of modular building and standardized modern components our decorating choices have become paradoxically freer. While some may groan at the lack of character in many modern rooms, a bland interior does have the advantage of offering adaptability. If you live in a spacious Georgian or Victorian house, the task of restoring it to its original perfection must take priority, and many of your design decisions will be foregone conclusions.

But given an interior that lacks a strong style of its own, you can choose to recreate a Japanese dining room, an early American bedroom or a modern living room without any period features to hinder you.

In planning this 'style' book, I have found that deciding on a dozen styles to single out has not been easy. Ultimately I have selected those which I believe to be today's favourites and which, within the context of

current trends and what is available on the market, are the easiest to translate into rooms of the size most of us live in today. Believing that cash restraints can be the origin of inventiveness, I have worked on the basis that no style is the sole prerogative of the fabulously rich. If you can't afford a mosaic floor you can fake one using stencils and, with a canvas and some paint, you can create your own version of a Kandinsky or a Mondrian, or dream up something original, that is entirely your own.

Each of the 12 looks is set out as a visual recipe, listing the ingredients and images needed to create that particular style. In each case, I have suggested alternative colour schemes to help you make the room your own. Throughout the book, I have included many

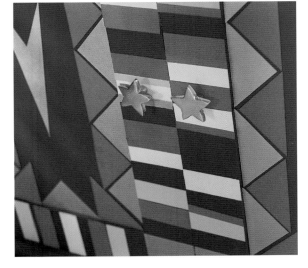

of the most ingenious decorating tricks I have learned over the years. Some of the projects are really simple – the kind you could attempt in a spare half hour – but once you have achieved successful results, they could provide the inspirational springboards to transforming a whole room. Despise not small beginnings.

Decorating has to be one of the most enjoyable aspects of home-making (some people prefer cooking, or even cleaning, I know) but I am assuming you share my enthusiasm. My prayer is that you will find at least one idea or style within this book to make your home sing with originality and beauty, and that you will enormously enjoy making it a reality.

Maggie Colvin

Techniques

Stencils

Stencil designs have been included for many of the room schemes, as they are a simple way to decorate walls, floors and furniture. Once you have mastered how to cut the stencils, you can develop your own designs, tailor-made to suit the size of your rooms. Alternatively, ready-cut designs are available from a wide range of sources.

First enlarge the stencils to the size required on a photocopier, then transfer onto stencil card or trace onto acetate sheet. Acetate usually lasts longer and is easy to clean and position, but card is slightly absorbent: if you apply too much paint the edges are less likely to smudge. The stencil can be cut out with a craft knife, or, if you are using acetate, a heat pen. Remember to rest the heat pen on a ceramic plate when not in use, so the tip is not in contact with the surface.

Making stencils

A craft knife is particularly suited to cutting straight edges and corners. Use a steel rule, held down firmly, and run the craft knife against it. However, a heat pen is good for curves, and the steps below show how to use one.

Step 1 To trace the stencil, tape a piece of tracing paper over the enlarged design and trace with a fine felt-tipped pen or soft pencil.

Step 2 To cut acetate with a heat pen, lay the tracing paper under a piece of glass and place a sheet of acetate, lightly coated with spray adhesive, on top of the glass. Fix the acetate firmly in place by taping around the edges. When the heat pen has warmed up, carefully draw over the acetate, following the outlines of the stencil. Move the heat pen steadily along the line. If you leave it to rest in one place for too long it will make a hole. Once the design is complete, remove the parts of the stencil. Some will fall out easily, others will need to be eased out with your fingers. Some may even need to be snipped with a small pair of sharp scissors.

Stencilling

STENCIL PAINTS ALLOW YOU MORE OPPORTUNITY
TO VARY TEXTURES AND COLOURS AS THEY CAN BE
APPLIED OVER THE STENCIL WITH SPONGES OR
SMALL ROLLERS AS WELL AS BRUSHES.

Step 1   Secure the stencil in place with
low-tack masking tape. Take up a small
amount of paint on the brush and dab off the
excess on a piece of paper towel. For a textured
effect, dab the brush over the holes of the
stencil; for a smoother finish, use a circular
brush stroke to apply the paint. Apply lighter
colours first, gradually building up darker
tones, and apply the colour consistently.

Step 2   To add depth and shade, dab the
brush in a second, brighter, colour. Here,
a darker green was applied along the
right-hand side of the leaves to balance
the highlights on the opposite side and
create a three-dimensional effect. If the
colours are too vibrant, leave to dry, then
go over the work with a thin wash of
gold or light brown.

Step 3   For a more hand-painted effect, paint
in bridges in the stencil in an appropriate
colour and add further details with a fine
brush. Here, the veins are being painted in a
pale green. After removing the stencil, you can
use a brush to add extra details and highlights
to suggest sunlight, or to add darker tones to
emphasise shade.

Paint Effects

T HE ROOM SCHEMES IN THIS BOOK RELY ON A COMBINATION OF ADAPTED FURNISHINGS, APPLIED PATTERNS SUCH AS STENCILS, CAREFULLY CHOSEN ACCESSORIES, AND APPROPRIATE COLOUR SCHEMES. CONSIDER USING ONE OF THE PAINT EFFECTS BELOW TO APPLY COLOUR TO YOUR WALLS.

Sponging

PROBABLY ONE OF THE QUICKEST AND EASIEST PAINT TECHNIQUES, SPONGING PRODUCES A FRESH-LOOKING SPATTERED EFFECT WHICH WORKS ON MOST SURFACES, EVEN ROUGH, UNEVEN TEXTURES SUCH AS WOODCHIP OR CONCRETE. A NATURAL SEA SPONGE WILL CREATE A MORE INTERESTING, IRREGULAR AND NATURAL TEXTURE THAN A SYNTHETIC SPONGE. THERE ARE TWO BASIC TECHNIQUES: SPONGING ON, WHICH IS SIMPLY SPONGING THE GLAZE DIRECTLY ONTO THE PAINTED SURFACE, AND SPONGING OFF, IN WHICH THE GLAZE IS APPLIED OVER A BASE COAT WITH A BRUSH, THEN LIFTED OFF WITH A SPONGE. TWO COLOURS CAN BE APPLIED TO CREATE A MORE TEXTURED EFFECT.

Step 1   To sponge on: Pour your chosen glaze into a saucer. Wet the sponge, then wring it out thoroughly so it is just damp. Dab the sponge into the glaze then dab it onto the wall. Do not twist the sponge as you make contact. Change the angle of the sponge to avoid repeat patterns. Work over the surface in this way. If you are applying a second, darker colour, apply the first colour lightly, allowing the base colour to show through.

Step 2   If you are applying a second colour, rinse the sponge thoroughly before applying the second layer of glaze. This can be done without waiting for the first coat to dry, unless you want the option of wiping off mistakes (if this is the case, apply a coat of clear varnish after the first and any subsequent coats). Apply the second glaze lightly, as before, remembering that your final colour will be dominant. Use a small artist's or stencil brush to get right into the corners of the room.

Step 3   To sponge off: For a denser effect and a more even-textured result, use a large brush to apply the glaze evenly and generously over the base coat. Using a damp sponge, dab over the glaze to remove the brush marks and to lift off some of the colour to reveal the base coat. Clean the sponge frequently in clear water, and vary the angle of your wrist as before. To sponge off glaze in the corners of the room, break off a small piece of sponge or use a stencil brush.

Stippling

THIS TECHNIQUE CREATES A SOPHISTICATED TEXTURED LOOK AND IS SIMPLE TO MASTER. STIPPLING LOOKS BEST ON A PERFECT SURFACE BECAUSE, UNLIKE WITH SPONGING OR COLOURWASHING, EVERY IMPERFECTION IS LIKELY TO SHOW THROUGH. TO SHOW UP PROPERLY, THE GLAZE NEEDS TO HAVE A HIGH CONCENTRATION OF COLOUR, AS IT SHOULD BE SPREAD FAIRLY THINLY. FOR RICHER EFFECTS, USE A DEEPLY COLOURED GLAZE OVER A BACKGROUND JUST A COUPLE OF SHADES PALER.

Step 1   Cover the base coat with a thin layer of glaze, brushing evenly in all directions. Go over the surface once more and, using the tip of the brush, gently push and disperse any heavy brush strokes and lumps of colour.

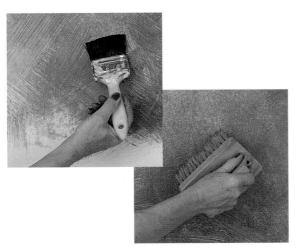

Step 2   Gripping the stippling brush firmly, hit the surface at a 90-degree angle with sharp, regular stabbing strokes. Do not move the brush across the glaze, as this will smudge it. Work in small sections: each time you move to a new area, stipple over the edge of the previous area to make sure the effect is consistent. Any specks of dust or air bubbles can be removed while the glaze is wet; stipple again immediately to restore the even texture.

Colourwashing

THIS TECHNIQUE IS QUICK TO APPLY AND, DEPENDING ON THE COLOURS YOU USE, ENORMOUSLY VERSATILE. IN STONE, GREY AND MAUVE IT CAN CREATE A CASUAL, CONTEMPORARY LOOK, WHILE IN TERRACOTTA AND EARTH TONES IT WILL GIVE A ROOM A RUSTIC FARMHOUSE FEEL. A DARK GREEN COLOURWASH MAKES A GOOD BACKDROP FOR ANTIQUE MAHAGONY FURNITURE WHILE DEEP REDS ARE PERFECT FOR A JAPANESE LOOK.

Step 1   Apply the glaze using a large brush, working in all directions over the area. Work on one section at at time, otherwise the glaze may dry out before you have time to finish the treatment. When the glaze is slightly tacky, wipe over the wall with a soft cloth scrunched up into a pad with a smooth surface. Wipe in all directions, exposing the base coat without removing the glaze altogether, until all brush marks are obliterated. Use different areas of the cloth as it becomes saturated, eventually replacing it with a clean one.

Step 2   For double colourwashing, leave the first coat to dry, then apply a second coat in the same way. Keep working until the glaze looks soft and evenly distributed. For an extra cloudy finish, use a softening brush. Hold it at 90 degrees to the surface, and flick over the surface with the action of a pendulum.

New England Bathroom

THE SEASIDE BEACH-HUT LOOK TOOK OFF WHEN

NEW YORKERS LOOKED TO THE NEW ENGLAND

SHORE FOR WEEKEND BREAKS, ALTHOUGH SHELL

CRAFTS HAVE BEEN DEVELOPED OVER

CENTURIES, AND WERE ESPECIALLY POPULAR

WITH THE VICTORIANS. TODAY THIS STYLE IS A

UNIVERSAL FAVOURITE, PARTICULARLY FOR

BATHROOMS. ENCAPSULATING VISUAL REMINDERS

OF THE SEA, IT REKINDLES FOND MEMORIES OF

HAPPY SUMMER HOLIDAYS AND NAUTICAL VENTURES.

Focus on Style

The 'oceana' look is a relaxed style which contains all the characteristic ingredients of the seashore. With its gentle sun-bleached colours and driftwood textures developed naturally from exposure to the sea, salt and sun, the look is simple, rustic and timeless as the sea itself.

Begin with a matt emulsion paint in a shade that conjures up a clear seascape sparkling in sunlight. Use unsealed wooden tongue-and-groove boards, laid horizontally and painted with dilute off-white emulsion, to echo the line of the horizon. Sanded, pale, bare floorboards are ideal for this beach-hut look. For an extremely practical floor you can emulate a yacht deck, with highly varnished narrow boards; some laminated wood plank copies are indistinguishable from the real thing.

Wooden shutters are eminently suitable. They can be left as they are or painted, dry-brushed or distressed. Jute, sailcloth and denim can be headed with white eyelets and threaded with manila rope to make nautical-style curtains.

Collect pebbles and shells and show them off in glass jars. For shell curtain hooks, drill a hole through the top of each shell, thread with a brass ring and attach to a curtain ring. To make pebble candlesticks, choose two or three pebbles with flat bottoms and drill a hole in each to match the diameter of a candle.

WALLS
Choose from a wide range of aquatic blues, including Aegean turquoise and pale clean greens. You could dilute intense colours with a scumble glaze to achieve a translucent effect. For a really peaceful colour scheme, make sure that a high proportion of the room surface is decorated in creamy white or pale sand to offset stronger accent colours.

FURNITURE
Choose driftwood textures or create your own by scouring untreated wood and brushing on a liming wax or diluted white emulsion, rubbed in the direction of the grain. Over a base coat of plain paint in the colour of the sea, dry-brush soft streaks of off-white to give wood a sun-bleached, salt-dried look.

FABRICS

Cotton fabrics, woven in wide stripes of blue and white or yellow and white, resemble the canvas traditionally used for Victorian beach tents and conjure up the seaside look. Striped voiles fall and move softly, as if blown by a warm summer sea breeze.

FLOORS

Brush bare boards with diluted emulsion in off-white, sand, pale turquoise or grey-blue, working along the grain, then protect the floorboards with several coats of floor varnish.

ACCESSORIES

Shells, pebbles, sand, rope and other beach finds are the essential ingredients. To echo a sun-bleached colour scheme, limed curtain rails and rope tie-backs and handles are a good choice, and seashells complete the look.

DETAILS

A large shell makes a perfect soap dish. Most fishmongers will sell scallop shells inexpensively and some might even have spares to give away.

Chest with Shell Handles

To create the texture of driftwood, dry-brushing is the best and simplest paint effect. You can try this on any piece of furniture: it works well over a smooth MDF base and even better over real wood, when it has the additional merit of bringing out the texture of the wood grain. Choose a sea blue for the base coat and dry-brush in off-white – the colour of dried sea salt. Pretty handles made of real seashells complete the look, though they are only practical for small, lightweight drawers.

Materials and equipment

small chest of drawers • matt emulsion paint in turquoise and off-white • medium decorator's paintbrush, preferably stiff and old • paper towels • sandpaper • epoxy resin, plaster or interior filler • 6 small rounded scallop or cockle shells of equal size • spoon • 6 pre-cut wooden dowels • ruler and pencil • electric drill with drill bit to match diameter of dowels • wood glue

Step 1 Paint the chest and drawer fronts with deep turquoise emulsion. Sand and apply a second coat if necessary. Leave to dry, then dip a dry brush sparingly into off-white emulsion and dab off the excess on paper towels. Draw the brush lightly over the turquoise, working in one direction only to create a 'driftwood' effect. Try not to overpaint, but if you do, wait for the paint to dry then rub down with sandpaper to even out the effect.

Step 2 Mix together the two parts of the epoxy resin (or mix some plaster or filler with water) and fill each shell.

Step 3 Push a dowel into the filler in each shell and leave to set. Find the middle of each drawer and mark it lightly with a pencil. Drill a hole about 5mm/¼in deep in each drawer.

Step 4 Blow away the sawdust and fill each hole with wood glue. Push the dowel in a shell handle into each hole and leave to set.

Rope Border

As the yachting world now relies almost entirely on nylon rope, thick old-style jute rope is hard to find and, if you are lucky enough to find old stock in a ship's chandlery, is expensive. But by using several strands of jute sash cord, twisted into one thick piece, you can create a similarly chunky effect. The knots that hold the strands together also add character to the border.

Materials and equipment

several hanks of jute sash cord • scissors • elastic bands • small furniture tacks and hammer • enough flat scallop shells to encircle the room • electric drill and fine drill bit

Step 1
Cut the sash cord into four equal lengths and hold them together at one end with an elastic band. Twist the strands together to create one thick rope.

Step 2 Tie a loose knot about every 30cm/12in, to keep the strands from separating. Continue twisting until you reach the end. Finish with a knot and cut away any loose ends carefully so that the knot does not fall apart. If more than one length of twisted, knotted rope is needed to encircle the room, more ropes can be created in the same way, and any joins hidden in the corners of the room or behind the knots.

Step 3 Secure the twisted, knotted rope along the top of the panelling on the wall using tacks and a hammer. If your room does not have panelling, use a spirit level and pencil to mark out a straight line at dado height and attach the rope along this.

Step 4 To attach the scallop shells, drill one hole in the top of each and one on either side at the bottom. Space the shells evenly and align the bottom of each one with the rope. Tack carefully to the wall. Make a second knotted rope as before and tack to the wall, lining it up with the tops of the shells.

Shell Mirror

Step 1 Prepare the frame using a stiff wire brush, rubbing along the direction of the grain to dislodge as much wood pulp as possible. Brush the surface with white emulsion and immediately wipe away the excess paint with a rag.

I F YOU DON'T HAVE A SUITABLE FRAMED MIRROR, OLD FLOORBOARDS, CUT TO SIZE AND MITRED TO MAKE INTO A FRAME, WOULD BE IDEAL FOR THIS PROJECT – THE MORE BATTERED THE BETTER. SOME FLOORBOARDS HAVE A GROOVED EDGE, WHICH MAKES AN EXCELLENT SLOT INTO WHICH TO FIT THE EDGE OF THE MIRROR. YOU CAN, OF COURSE, USE ANY ARRANGEMENT OF SHELLS, DEPENDING ON THE TYPES IN YOUR COLLECTION.

Step 2 Using a glue gun, squeeze glue around the outside edge of each scallop shell and position around the sides and the bottom of the frame. Glue the three whelk shells at the top, butting the narrow ends together to form a fan shape.

Wall Sconce

C ANDLES ARE A ROMANTIC BONUS IN A BATHROOM, AND THIS PROJECT IS A PARTICULARLY SAFE AND PRETTY WAY TO INCORPORATE THEM. IT CAN ALSO BE USED AS A SOAP DISH. INSTEAD OF USING THE CUPBOARD RAIL-HOLDER SUGGESTED, YOU MIGHT FIND A WROUGHT-IRON BRACKET IN A JUNK SHOP, OR YOU COULD EVEN USE AN OLD BATHROOM TUMBLER HOLDER.

Materials and equipment

two round scallop shells • electric drill with fine drill bit • picture wire and wire cutters • cupboard rail-holder • screws and screwdriver • epoxy resin glue • candle

Step 1 Drill a hole on either side of the base of each scallop shell. Drill a further hole in the centre of the shell that will form the back of the sconce. Cut a length of picture wire and thread it through the two lower holes in each shell to hold them with the bottom edges butted together. Twist the wire to secure it.

Step 2 Screw the cupboard rail-holder to the wall. Position the shells so that the lower one sits on the ring of the rail-holder.

Step 3 Glue the base of the lower shell to the rail-holder and screw the back of the sconce to the wall. Sit a candle in place.

Country Breakfast Room

Traditionally, country cottages were

humble homes for farmworkers. Today the

style represents a rural dream – a cherished

promise of a peaceful escape from the

fast-moving, competitive life of the city. The

cottage idiom is fresh, simple, unpretentious,

warm, charming and pretty. It can even appeal

to city-dwellers in high-rise blocks,

especially for creating cosy kitchens

and romantic bedrooms.

Focus on Style

The key architectural elements are window seats, beams, inglenooks and low ceilings: all these can be simulated within the context of a modern structure. With distressed paint effects, most new surfaces can be transformed to look time-worn and softly patinated.

The key to country cottage style lies in choosing 'country' colours. Intense colours – which historically contained expensive pigments – should be avoided. Wallpapers with small-scale designs are a relatively modern invention but they can create a 'busy' look that will help to reproduce a lived-in atmosphere. Stencils are a more authentic way of introducing pattern. Any existing natural textures, such as brick, wooden panelling or rough rendering, are a bonus and should be exposed, cleaned up and sealed or painted. Wall-to-wall carpet may feel cosy, but carpets and rugs did not come easily within the average cottager's budget.

WALLS
Country-style colours range from pretty soft pastels to muted earthy autumnal colours – leaf greens, ochre, apricot and terracotta. White walls are typical, but pale primrose yellow would add warmth.

Country cottage furniture would have been passed down through generations, so second-hand furniture is ideal. Nothing should look modern or contrived. Any newly painted furniture should be aged or distressed, but natural woods like dark oak and antique pine are typical. Cottage furniture was always made from locally available, inexpensive materials.

An individual mix of fabrics and colours helps to create a look of homely clutter. Old throws and shawls, hand-embroidered or tapestry cushions and hand-made quilts are evidence of the skilled, busy fingers of generations of country-born people.

FABRICS

Mini geometric and floral prints work well together in small rooms: checks add freshness to old-fashioned roses, which are an intrinsic part of the look. Simple rope tassels and plain white bobble fringes are suitably unsophisticated.

FLOORS

Choose simple and inexpensive-looking rugs laid on natural materials. Typical cottage floors were nearly always in stone, brick or quarry tiles.

ACCESSORIES

Black iron latch door handles and wooden curtain poles, natural or painted, are key details. Unsophisticated rustic wooden mouldings can be successfully superimposed on modern pine panelling and doors.

Display Shelves

To give new paintwork a seasoned look, use candle wax to hamper the adherence of water-based paint so that it can be distressed with sandpaper. In this way you can imitate the look of a surface where the top layer of paint has worn away in places – usually at the edges and in areas of high use, such as around the handles – to reveal the undercoat. The candle can also be used to draw dates and initials, as country pieces were often personalised to record family weddings. Different colourways produce different effects. A terracotta base coat is a well-tried choice, as it will give the piece a warm glow, and cosy warmth captures the spirit of cottage style.

Step 1 Seal the bare wood or MDF with a coat of PVA glue or white primer. Leave to dry then sand smooth. Apply the terracotta base coat and leave to dry again.

Step 2 Rub a household candle over the edges of the furniture and in places such as the area around the drawer knob – spots which would naturally receive the most wear and tear. Draw a love-heart and appropriate initials, using the candle like a pencil.

Step 3 Apply a top coat of pale duck egg blue emulsion and leave to dry.

Materials and equipment
wooden display shelf unit •
PVA glue or white wood primer •
medium decorator's paintbrush •
medium and coarse sandpaper •
matt emulsion paint in terracotta
and pale duck-egg blue •
household candle • beeswax
or brush-on furniture wax and
soft cloth

Step 4 Rub away the final coat, using coarse sandpaper to begin with, concentrating on the areas previously waxed. As you do so, areas of terracotta will begin to show through.

Step 5 Apply a final coat of beeswax or clear furniture wax to give the piece an extra patina.

Fabric Vase

Materials and equipment

chintz remnant • scissors • cardboard box (such as a shoebox) • pins • sewing machine and matching thread • needle • PVA glue • decorator's paintbrush • jam jar

Step 2 Put the fabric back on the box. Turn the box upside down and wrap the fabric over the bottom as if you were wrapping a paper parcel. Pin, then slipstitch together.

T HIS IS AN ORIGINAL AND SIMPLE WAY TO INJECT MORE FLORAL IMAGES INTO THE ROOM AND ENJOY YOUR FAVOURITE CHINTZES IN SMALL, AFFORDABLE PIECES. IT IS ALSO A GOOD WAY TO USE UP FABRIC OFFCUTS. ONCE FOLDED AND STITCHED INTO A BOX SHAPE, THE FABRIC IS STIFFENED WITH PVA GLUE. TO CONTAIN THE WATER AND FLOWERS, YOU WILL NEED A SIMPLE CONTAINER SUCH AS A JAM JAR: AS THIS WILL BE COMPLETELY HIDDEN IT DOESN'T MATTER WHAT IT LOOKS LIKE.

Step 3 Apply two or three coats of PVA glue to the sides and base of the vase, leaving the glue to dry between coats. Remove the box. Place an old jam jar or kitchen storage jar within the vase to contain the water and flowers.

Step 1 Cut a piece of fabric big enough to wrap around the sides and bottom of the box. Wrap the fabric, wrong side out, around the box and pin the side edges together. Fold a double 5mm/¼in hem around the top edge and pin. Remove the fabric from the box and machine stitch the side seam and top hem. Press the seams and turn right side out.

Crackle-effect Table

THIS IS A SIMPLE RECIPE WHICH CAN BE APPLIED DIRECTLY TO BARE NEW PINE TO AGE IT. BEGIN WITH A SMALL TEST AREA – PREFERABLY OUT OF SIGHT – UNDER OR AT THE BACK OF THE TABLETOP. IF THE PINE LOOKS PARTICULARLY NEW AND BRIGHT, IT WOULD BE WISE TO DULL IT DOWN FIRST WITH A COAT OF DIRTY YELLOW EMULSION PAINT, THINNED 1:1 WITH WATER.

Step 1 Make sure the wood surface is clean and dry. Apply the crackle glaze as evenly as possible and in one direction only. Make sure you do not brush over the same area twice. Leave to dry completely.

Step 2 Apply off-white emulsion paint over the crackle glaze in one direction only, and as smoothly and evenly as possible. Do not brush over the same area twice.

Step 3 The crackle effect will appear as the paint dries. To achieve a more marked effect, you can speed up the drying process using a hairdryer. When the paint is dry, protect the surface with several coats of matt acrylic varnish.

Stencilled Floor

**Materials
and equipment**
*cream vinyl silk emulsion
paint • large paintbrush •
string • drawing pins •
pencil • photocopier •
acetate for stencils •
glass sheet or cutting
mat • masking tape •
hot pen or craft knife •
spray adhesive •
straight edge • stencil
paint in light and
dark green • 2 stencil
brushes • paper towel •
floor varnish •
varnishing brush*

A S AN INEXPENSIVE MEANS OF DECORATION, STENCILLING PAINTED FLOORBOARDS HAS BEEN POPULAR ALL OVER EUROPE FOR CENTURIES. USING A STRAIGHT BORDER LIKE THIS SIMPLE LEAF DESIGN, WITH A CO-ORDINATING CORNER PIECE, YOU CAN GIVE THE ROOM A REAL COUNTRY FEEL. A GOOD FLOOR VARNISH IS ESSENTIAL: WITH THIS PROTECTION, THE FLOOR SHOULD STAY FRESH AND PRETTY FOR SEVERAL YEARS.

Step 1 Paint the floor with two coats of cream vinyl silk emulsion paint. When dry, find the centre of the room using two pieces of string, fixed diagonally across the room with drawing pins in the corners. Mark the point where they cross. Decide on the size of the square pattern and draw it on the floor using a pencil and straight edge. Photocopy and enlarge the leaf and corner designs opposite, and cut the stencils from acetate sheets.

Step 2 Spray the back of the corner stencil with adhesive and place it on the centre point. Paint this first, beginning with the lighter shade of green, then work outwards from the centre along the marked lines using the border stencil.

Step 3 Apply the darker shade to the centre of each stencil to create depth and texture. To ensure the brush is not overloaded, twist it on a paper towel before painting.

Step 4 When you reach the edge of the room, use masking tape to mask off the leaf stencil where necessary. Finish by placing the border stencil close to the skirting board and use the corner design to complete the squares. Apply several coats of floor varnish following the manufacturer's instructions.

enlarge by 30%

enlarge by 15%

Mexican Dining Room

THE MEXICAN LOOK DRAWS ON A WIDE RANGE

OF INFLUENCES FROM INCA, SPANISH AND

FRENCH CULTURES, AND IS AS COLOURFUL AND

DEMONSTRATIVE AS MEXICAN CULTURE ITSELF.

INTENSELY HAPPY, BRIGHT COLOURS, WITH

SIMPLE DECORATIVE SHAPES, MAKE IT EASY TO

RE-CREATE. NOT A STYLE FOR THE FAINT-HEARTED,

IT PROVIDES LIVELY INSPIRATION FOR THIS

DRAMATIC DINING ROOM.

Focus on Style

A mixture of bright colours – think chrome yellow, midnight blue, hot red, purple and pink, and some silver – is essential to this look. The simplest way to combine this closely woven palette is by painting frames or chairs in different colours, or by introducing a simple zig-zag border to encircle a window, or edge the top of the room. Simple folk-style shapes such as triangular patterns, stripes and dots, are appropriately unsophisticated. Dark-stained rustic wooden furniture – instead of the brightly painted taverna chairs shown here – would tone down the room if you wished.

Approach your colour choices bravely. Remember that once the furniture and accessories are in place, sizzling pink will appear to recede and will not seem as overpowering as it does when you apply the first coat. To mellow the intensity, you could add a glaze to the paint and apply a colourwash. To create a roughly textured wall, add some fine-textured interior filler to the paint: combine one part filler with two parts emulsion paint and mix slowly and thoroughly.

A few ethnic folk objects, like a collection of large stone jars, tin frames, lanterns and candlesticks, or feathers and beads in bright colours, provide light-hearted finishing touches to the Mexican look. An eclectic mix of textiles such as shawls and cushions is exported from Mexico and is widely available.

WALLS
Use a pallette of brave eye-catching colours. Colourwash walls to create a textured effect.

FABRICS
The most vividly coloured fabrics available cheaply on the market today are silks dyed in India. Brilliant fabrics look exuberant draped over a curtain pole or thrown over a sofa. Stripes and kilim designs look typically Mexican, as does silk sewn with mirror sequins and embroidered cottons.

FLOORS
For the floor, dark wood stain, sisal or clay tiles convey the style best. In a room with dark walls, a much lighter floor is important as it will create a dramatic contrast between the dark and light, which like sun and shadow suggests a bright climate.

ACCESSORIES
To add some welcome sparkle amidst the dense bright colours, silver accessories, picture frames, beads, handles and tassels are vital ingredients, injecting light and life. Mexican tinware is traditional to the culture.

Painted Border

STRICTLY IN THE FOLK-ART TRADITION, WALL DECORATIONS SHOULD BE BASED ON UNSOPHISTICATED GEOMETRIC SHAPES, APPLIED IN A FREE, UNINHIBITED FASHION. USING A TOOTHBRUSH IS REMARKABLY EFFECTIVE, BECAUSE THE BRISTLES CREATE INSTANT STRAIGHT, BOLD LINES. FOR CLEAN-SHAPED DOTS, JUST TURN A COMPLETE CIRCLE ON THE SPOT USING AN ORDINARY 1CM/½IN PAINTBRUSH. YOU CAN USE THIS KIND OF BORDER DECORATION TO FRAME ALCOVES, DOORS, WINDOWS OR ANY ARCHITECTURAL FEATURE.

Materials and equipment

masking tape • turquoise matt emulsion paint • medium and 1cm/½in decorator's paintbrushes • set square and pencil • acrylic paint in silver and purple • old saucer • toothbrush • eraser • acrylic varnish • varnish brush

Step 1 Mask a 15cm/6in wide border around the window frame and paint with turquoise emulsion paint. Leave to dry. Using a set square and pencil, draw a zig-zag pattern around the window. Adjust the size and angle of the pattern to fit as neatly as possible.

Step 2 Pour some silver paint into a saucer and dip a toothbrush flat into the paint. Brush along the pencil lines. Pull the toothbrush smoothly towards you. Keep the toothbrush flat as you move it and exert an even, constant pressure so that the width of the line remains fairly consistent.

Step 3 Paint in the purple dots inside each triangle by holding a 1cm/½in brush at a 90 degree angle to the wall and making a 360 degree turn on the spot. If you make a mistake, wipe it off quickly with a damp cloth. Leave to dry before beginning again.

Step 4 When the paint is dry, use an eraser to carefully rub away any pencil lines still showing round the border. To protect the finished decoration, apply a coat of acrylic varnish.

Striped Sideboard

I F YOU CAN'T AFFORD AN AUTHENTIC ANTIQUE
CARVED SIDEBOARD, YOU CAN STILL GIVE PLAIN
FURNITURE A MEXICAN LOOK. THIS TECHNIQUE IS
A RELATIVELY QUICK WAY TO DECORATE AN MDF
CUPBOARD. CUTTING SHAPES OUT OF BRIGHTLY
COLOURED CARD IS MUCH QUICKER THAN HAND-PAINTING
GEOMETRIC DESIGNS, AND IT'S AN EASY WAY TO
ACHIEVE CRISP LINES. PAINT THE CUPBOARD FIRST IN
A DEEP PURPLE-BLUE, THEN SPACE THE CARD SHAPES
SO THAT THE BLUE GAPS REGISTER AS EXTRA STRIPES.

Materials and equipment
*MDF sideboard with panelled doors • midnight blue
emulsion paint • decorator's paintbrush • sandpaper •
selection of brightly coloured card, including silver, yellow,
lime green, orange, and red • pencil • cutting mat,
steel rule and craft knife • spray adhesive • wallpaper
paste • acrylic varnish • varnish brush • 2 star-shaped
door knobs*

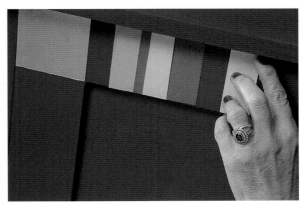

Step 1 Paint the cupboard with two coats of midnight blue emulsion, sanding between coats. Leave to dry. Measure the width of the door frames and draw eight squares on the silver card to fit into the corners. Cut them out and stick in position using spray adhesive.

Step 2 Cut strips from all the different colours of card, matching the width of the door frames and varying the width of the strips. Juxtapose the colours for contrast and stick in position to create a striped edge. Leave some gaps of plain blue paint.

Step 3 Measure the height of the recessed panels and divide the measurement by four. Cut four silver triangles to this measurement and stick them along each panel edge. Cut a silver triangle for the top and bottom of each panel. Cut red triangles the same size and stick inside the zig-zag shape formed by the line of silver triangles. Leave narrow gaps between them to form blue outlines. Cut short strips of card to stick along the top edge of the sideboard.

Step 4 Using the picture opposite as a guide, cut two silver arrow shapes. Glue and centre on the door fronts. Stick down any loose pieces of card using wallpaper paste and leave to settle. Finish with several coats of acrylic varnish, allowing each coat to dry thoroughly. Finally, attach a star-shaped knob to each door.

Curtain-pole Candlesticks

I F YOU'VE RECENTLY SWAPPED YOUR OLD WOODEN
CURTAIN POLES FOR SLIM METAL RODS, THIS IS AN
INGENIOUS WAY OF UTILIZING A STOCK OF LEFTOVER
HOLDERS, FINIALS AND WOODEN CURTAIN RINGS, BY
TURNING THEM INTO 'CARVED' CANDLESTICKS THAT
YOU CAN PAINT IN MEXICAN COLOURS. YOU'LL ALSO
NEED THE KIND OF STOUT CARDBOARD TUBE THAT IS
USED TO HOLD ROLLS OF FURNISHING FABRIC.

Materials and equipment

*cardboard tube • jigsaw • matt emulsion paint in
midnight blue and several bright colours • decorator's
paintbrush • curtain rings, holders and finials • MDF
offcuts • screws and screwdriver • glue gun • gravel or
sand • candles*

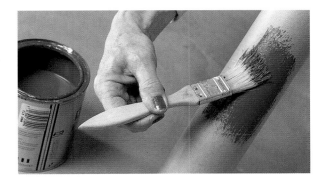

Step 1 Cut lengths of cardboard tube to the desired finished height of each candlestick and paint with midnight blue emulsion. Leave to dry and apply a second coat if necessary.

Step 2 Saw the finials and holders where necessary to flatten their bases. Use to make a bottom section and a candleholder for each candlestick. Screw the base on to a square plinth cut from MDF.

Step 3 Paint the tops, bottoms and curtain rings in a range of bright colours. You may find the rings are easier to spray than to paint with a brush.

Step 4 Fit a length of cardboard tube over each base and glue in place. Fill the tube with gravel or sand to give it stability.

Step 5 Slot the curtain rings over the tube and glue to the base.

Step 6 Glue a candleholder to the top of each tube and insert a candle.

Papier Mâché Bowl

THIS MEXICAN BOWL IS A LESS FRAGILE DECORATIVE SUBSTITUTE FOR REAL POTTERY AND IT'S A PROJECT THAT'S EASY ENOUGH EVEN FOR CHILDREN TO TACKLE. YOU CAN BUY READY-MADE PAPIER MÂCHÉ PULP WHICH YOU SIMPLY MIX WITH WATER, OR MAKE YOUR OWN FROM PAPER TORN INTO SMALL PIECES AND SOAKED IN WATER, WITH INTERIOR FILLER AND PVA GLUE ADDED. INSTEAD OF CACTUS SHAPES, YOU MIGHT PREFER TO DECORATE THE BOWL WITH BIRDS OR STARS.

Materials and equipment

paper hanging-basket liner • circular cardboard box lid, or stiff card strip • glue gun • marker pen • papier mâché pulp • interior filler • PVA glue • mixing bowl • decorator's paintbrush • white emulsion paint • acrylic paints in a selection of bright colours • artist's brush • matt acrylic varnish • varnish brush

Step 1 Glue a round box lid to the base of the hanging basket liner, using a glue gun, to make a foot for the bowl. (Alternatively, join the ends of a strip of card and glue this ring to the bowl.)

Step 2 Using a marker pen, draw four cactus shapes, equally spaced around the outside of the bowl. Fill each shape with papier mâché pulp and leave to dry.

Step 3 Mix interior filler with PVA glue and water to the consistency of yoghurt. Brush this mixture all over the bowl to smooth the surface. Leave to dry.

Step 4 Paint the bowl with a base coat of white emulsion. When this is dry, decorate in bright colours. Draw in the spines on the cacti using the marker pen. Seal the surface with several coats of acrylic varnish.

Modern
Living
Room

The ultimate in modern chic is still the

clutter-free, open-plan living space, which

represents today's contemporary lifestyle.

It is a crisp, fresh look that defies the

boundaries imposed by four square walls. It is

hi-tech and always evolving, with adaptable

and dramatic stage-set lighting, simple

ergonomic shapes and easy-to-clean surfaces.

Focus on Style

The current vogue is for purist lines and streamlined, hard-edged shapes. Metal and glass predominate against a backdrop of plain painted walls. Industrial flooring materials – such as sheet aluminium and studded synthetic rubber – are top of the purist's list. Clutter is outlawed so as not to detract from the feeling of spaciousness, augmented by reflective surfaces and clever lighting. Uplighters set behind a screen explode space in a dark corner, while a curtain of fairy lights behind a voile hanging suggests the existence of a lively urban skyline, as if viewed from a New York penthouse apartment.

A combination of voiles and plain blinds dictates the simplest, most functional window treatments. Taut wire curtain fittings and large cleat headings typify the minimal detailing this style will accommodate.

Stylish light fittings have assumed the status of sculpture. The pared-down style shuns fussy ornaments, and visual interest is as likely to be supplied by a shapely bottle off the supermarket shelf, sprayed silver or black or filled with coloured water, as by expensive Lalique glass. You might create your own abstract painting, or transform a fish tank into a stylish vase, filled with fresh flowers in a single strong colour.

WALLS
White walls have long been de rigueur, but other cool colours, such as chrome, grey, lime and aqua, have crept in. Intrinsic to any contemporary style are ever-shifting trends and constantly evolving fashions. Textured metallic papers and metallic paints are now making an impact.

FLOORS
Inconspicuous, neutral colours such as cream, beige or grey, in finely textured weaves, sisal and plain laminated wooden floors, provide a unifying basis to spartan simplicity.

FABRICS
The fashion for shimmering metallic voile fabrics reflects the sleekness of contemporary style. Patterns, such as circles, blocks and stripes, all in simple textures, are increasingly popular. They help to create a spacious feel in the way that busier, more complicated patterns do not.

ACCESSORIES
Introduce a note of fun with original resin or metallic door handles and glittering beaded coasters.

Modern Living Room 47

Metallic Screen

IN PREFERENCE TO A STRAIGHT SCREEN, CHOOSE
ONE WITH A STEPPED, CURVED TOP WHICH
CREATES SOFT SCULPTURAL LINES TO LESSEN THE
BOXY CHARACTER OF MANY MODERN ROOMS. PLACING
A TALL PLANT AND CONCEALED UPLIGHTERS BEHIND
THE SCREEN IS A GOOD WAY TO LIGHT THE CORNER OF
THE ROOM AND CREATE A FEELING OF EXTRA SPACE.

Materials and equipment
*MDF screen with curved top • about 20 cards, a
little larger than sheets of Dutch metal leaf • spray
adhesive • silver spray paint • masking tape • acrylic
gold size • 25-leaf pack of aluminium Dutch metal or
silver leaf • soft cloth • acrylic varnish • varnish brush*

Step 1 Glue the cards temporarily to the screen using a little spray adhesive, arranging them in a loosely stepped formation.

Step 2 Outside, or in a well-ventilated space, spray the screen silver, covering the MDF quite patchily to create a subtle shaded effect.

Step 3 Remove the cards to reveal the unpainted squares below. Mask around each square with masking tape and paint with acrylic gold size.

Step 4 Leave until the size feels tacky (this usually takes about 5–10 minutes) then apply the aluminium or silver leaf.

Step 5 Rub over the backing paper thoroughly with a soft cloth before peeling it away. Leave for 24 hours to dry, then finish with a protective coat of acrylic varnish applied over the whole screen.

Abstract Painting

Step 1 Form a cross shape on the canvas using 7.5cm/3in masking tape, positioning the cross about one-third of the way across the canvas.

Step 2 Using a small roller, roll green emulsion paint patchily over the two opposite corners. Use a sponge to apply aqua paint in the remaining corners.

P AINTING BLOCKS OF COLOUR ON A CANVAS DIVIDED BY STRIPES IS AN EFFECTIVE WAY TO BRING TOGETHER ALL THE COLOURS IN THE ROOM AND ADD A FEW SURPRISE SHADES. AN EVEN SIMPLER IDEA WOULD BE TO PAINT SEPARATE CANVASES IN DIFFERENT COLOURS AND HANG THEM AS A GROUP TO MAKE AN INTERESTING JUXTAPOSITION OF COLOURS. FOR A TEXTURED EFFECT, TRY APPLYING THE DIFFERENT PAINTS USING A SPONGE AND A SMALL ROLLER.

Materials and equipment
artist's canvas 60 x 90cm/24 x 36in • masking tape in 7.5cm/3in and 2.5cm/1in widths • matt emulsion paint in lime green, aqua, red and lilac • small paint roller and tray • natural sponge • decorator's paintbrush • 1cm/½in artist's brush

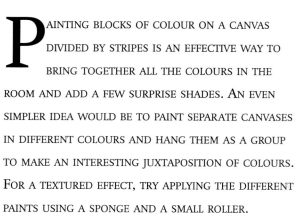

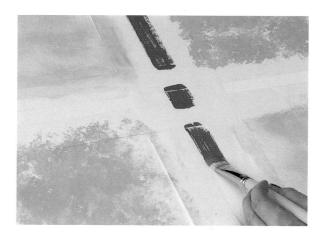

Step 3 Remove the masking tape and allow the paint to dry. Mask off the painted corners and apply the narrower tape within the cross shape. Using an artist's brush, paint different coloured stripes at random.

Step 4 Remove the tapes and re-mask to add further coloured stripes until you have the look you want.

Sparkling Curtain

Step 2 Cut around the pencil line. You may find it easier to cut an accurate circle if you fold the fabric in half as shown.

Step 3 Open the eyelet and place one half under the voile, tucking the raw edges into the lip. Press the top of the eyelet onto the lower half to secure the voile. Repeat for the remaining eyelets, spacing them 15cm/6in apart.

G IVE YOUR WINDOW AN IRRESISTIBLY GLITZY TREATMENT WITH AN EXCITING COMBINATION OF MODERN MATERIALS. THIS MESH OF TINY LIGHTS CAN BE STRETCHED RIGHT ACROSS A WINDOW, AND SPARKLES PRETTILY THROUGH A VOILE CURTAIN HANGING FROM GIANT SILVERED EYELETS.

Materials and equipment

length of voile to fit window, plus extra for hem and double heading • pins • sewing machine and matching thread • iron • large silvered plastic eyelets • pencil • small sharp-pointed scissors • aluminium curtain pole and brackets • fairy-light mesh

Step 1 Hem the bottom of the fabric in the usual way. At the top of the curtain, turn over the raw edge twice. Pin and press flat. Place an eyelet on the double hem and draw around the inside edge using a pencil.

Step 4 Thread the eyelets onto the pole and attach the mesh of lights behind the curtain, using the ties provided.

Framed Leaves

Step 2 Spray the assembled stand silver and leave to dry.

Step 3 Cut a piece of tracing paper to match the size of the glass, and arrange the spray of leaves on it. Sandwich between the two layers of glass.

T HIS STRIKING DECORATION IS SIMPLY MADE BY SANDWICHING A SPRAY OF FRESH LEAVES BETWEEN TWO SHEETS OF GLASS AND TRANSLUCENT PAPER. IN TIME, THE EDGES OF THE LEAVES MAY DISCOLOUR SLIGHTLY, BUT THEY ARE EASY TO REPLACE, BY SIMPLY UNCLIPPING THE CURTAIN CLIPS WHICH HOLD THE GLASS TOGETHER AT THE TOP.

Step 4 Slot the glass into the groove in the stand and position the curtain clip at the top to hold the layers together. For the best effect, place the picture in front of a small spotlight.

Materials and equipment

28cm/11in or 23cm/9in length of tongue-and-groove floorboard • pencil and ruler • saw • electric drill • wood glue • screws and screwdriver • silver spray paint • tracing paper • scissors • spray of leaves • 2 pieces of glass with polished edges, 28 x 23cm/11 x 9in • star curtain clips

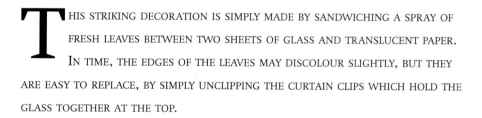

Step 1 Rule a straight line 2.5cm/1in away from the grooved edge of the floorboard and saw along the pencil line. Cut a piece 7.5cm/3in wide from the remaining piece of board. Glue and screw the grooved piece to the wider piece of board, working from the underside.

Flower Tank

Step 1 Cut a square of aluminium sheet to fit over the top of the glass tank, adding 1cm/½in all the way round. Cut a sheet of paper to the same size as the top of the tank and draw a grid over it. Place the aluminium sheet on the polystyrene with the paper pattern on top. Press a sharp pencil or wooden skewer through the paper at each point on the grid to perforate the sheet with stalk-size holes.

F LOWERS ARRANGED IN SEVERE, REGIMENTED STYLES SUIT A MODERN SETTING AND MAKE A STRONG COLOUR STATEMENT. GERBERAS AND TULIPS ARE IDEAL FOR THIS KIND OF DESIGN. BY MAKING A PERFORATED LID FOR A GLASS TANK, YOU CAN ARRANGE THE FLOWERS SO THAT THEY LOOK AS IF THEY ARE STILL GROWING IN NEAT ROWS.

Step 2 Centre the aluminium sheet over the top of the tank and fold down the overlapping edges to make a lid. Fold in the corners neatly. Lift off the lid to fill the vase with water. Cut all the flower stems to the same length and slot one into each hole.

Materials and equipment

square glass tank • sheet of lightweight embossing aluminium • paper • ruler and pencil • scissors • expanded polystyrene sheet • wooden skewer (optional) • gerberas or tulips

Early American Bedroom

The first European settlers in North America took a few treasured pieces of furniture to their new homes, but soon developed a distinctive decorative style of their own, interpreting the traditions of the countries they had left behind using local materials. Simple carpentry, homespun fabrics and painted decorations set the style which, with their legendary patchwork, has refreshed, enriched and inspired other cultures ever since. Today, it is the perfect inspiration for a country bedroom.

Focus on Style

Stencilled walls, natural floors, simple furniture and unpretentious window treatments using shutters and tab-headed curtains are typical of early American style. The atmosphere was spare but comfortable, with the 'waste not – want not' philosophy of the settlers outstandingly illustrated in their ravishing patchwork and embroidery. The most austere style of all was adopted by the Shakers, a Christian sect who believed that beauty and usefulness should go hand-in-hand. Minimal without being barren, the Shaker room had a plain wooden floor and walls of whitewashed or limed wood cladding, encircled by a row of pegs at picture-rail height. Chairs as well as hats and coats were hung from the pegs.

On walls, off-white, cream, and natural colours made a backdrop to stencilled patterns used as all-over designs or borders to outline interesting features, simulate a cornice or suggest a picture rail. Walls were sometimes timber-clad or roughly plastered and then limewashed. Wide, scrubbed wooden floorboards, stone or slate were typical of the early American style. Laminated floorboards are a perfect modern substitute and can look just like limed oak.

Homespun fabrics, as well as scraps of printed dress fabrics, were recycled to make patchwork quilts. To save time and effort, lots of companies now produce ready-made patchwork. Stencilling similar designs straight on to a quilt is an effective way to imitate the real thing.

WALLS
Walls were often covered in tongue-and-groove boarding with stencilled patterns to highlight interesting features or simulate a cornice or frieze. White or cream is best as a background colour for stencils. Use toning shades to create the stencil designs.

FABRICS

Crisp checks in red or blue and white are associated with early American country style. Quilts were decorated in a rich variety of traditional geometric designs.

Many companies now produce cream, textured Jaquard weaves in simple shaker-style patterns, which make ideal bedspreads and throws. Others make ready printed patchwork in padded textures. Embroidered borders were often added to curtains, bedcovers, clothes and cushions.

FLOORS

Laminated floorboards, or even real wood, make a perfect substitute for the scrubbed, sun bleached floorboards typical of early American dwellings. Old boards can be sanded and limed with a 50/50 mixture of water and white emulsion. Seal with a good matt floor varnish to protect.

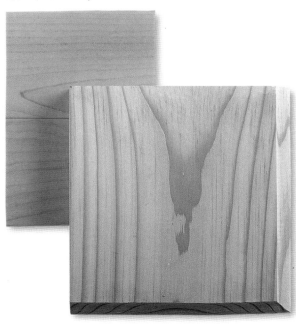

DETAILS

Simple cotton, such as broderie anglaise, was often made into café curtains and combined with shutters.

Stencilled Cupboard

*unpainted pine
cupboard • masking
tape • off-white
emulsion paint •
decorator's paintbrush •
pine-coloured glaze •
vase and border stencils
(see page 63) •
photocopier • spray
adhesive • oil stencil
crayons in yellow, red,
emerald green and
blue • scrap paper
or card • 4 stencil
brushes • acrylic
varnish • varnish brush*

THE SHOPS ARE FULL OF PLAIN MODERN CUPBOARDS THAT CAN BE GIVEN CHARACTER WITH A STENCILLED DESIGN. NEW, UNTREATED PINE CAN BE DARKENED WITH A GLAZE TO GIVE IT A MORE ANTIQUE LOOK. THIS CUPBOARD WAS AN INEXPENSIVE FLAT-PACK PURCHASE WHICH, WITH THE HELP OF OFF-WHITE PAINT AND TRADITIONAL STENCILS, WAS TRANSFORMED TO REPLICATE THE EARLY AMERICAN STYLE.

Step 1 Mask off the outer frame of the cupboard doors and apply a coat of off-white emulsion paint to the inner panels. If necessary, apply a second coat and leave to dry.

Step 2 Mask the painted panels and paint the frames in the pine-coloured glaze to dull the new wood. Leave to dry.

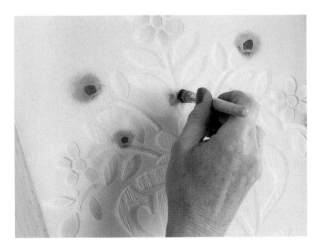

Step 3 Decide on the spacing of the stencils in the door panels and enlarge on a photocopier to fit. Apply spray adhesive to the back of the vase stencil and position. Rub some oil crayon on a sheet of scrap paper or card and pick up the colour with a stencil brush. Apply yellow to the flower heads, red to the buds and emerald green to the stems and leaves. Use blue for the vase.

Step 4 Repeat the process until the panels are covered. Finish with the small border design, positioning it to frame the vases. Leave for 24 hours to dry, as the crayons are oil-based and will run unless properly cured. Apply two coats of protective varnish to finish. Use the large border design to embellish the sides of the cupboard.

Peg Board

Materials and equipment
1cm/½in diameter wooden dowelling • saw • sandpaper • tape measure • pencil • 7.5 x 1cm/3 x ½in timber planks to encircle the room • electric drill with 1cm/½in drill bit • wood glue • screws and screwdriver

A LMOST EVERY SHAKER ROOM HAD A CONTINUOUS ROW OF PEGS ENCIRCLING THE ROOM AT PICTURE-RAIL HEIGHT FROM WHICH TO HANG CLOTHES, STORAGE SACKS AND EVEN CHAIRS. THIS DESIGN COULD BE MADE FROM OLD FLOORBOARDS SAWN IN TWO, OR JUST A NARROW PLANK, WITH DOWELLING CUT TO HOOK SIZE AND GLUED INTO PRE-DRILLED HOLES.

Step 1 Cut the dowelling into 6cm/2½in lengths and sand the cut edges smooth. Mark the positions for the pegs, about 15cm/6in apart, down the centre of the planks and drill the holes using a 1cm/½in drill bit.

Step 2 Glue the dowelling pegs into the holes. Screw the pre-drilled planks to the walls at picture-rail height, or along the top of timber cladding.

Stencilled Quilt

Materials and equipment

plain white cotton quilt • spray adhesive • 3 stencils (see page 63) • oil stencil crayons in red, blue, yellow, emerald and olive green • scrap paper or card • 5 stencil brushes • tape measure • pins • white tape • needle and matching thread

F ABRICS PRINTED IN TRADITIONAL QUILT DESIGNS ARE AVAILABLE TO BUY, BUT IF YOU CAN FIND A READY-QUILTED WHITE FABRIC, IT WILL MAKE AN IDEAL BACKGROUND FOR STENCILLED SQUARES REMINISCENT OF AMERICAN PATCHWORK. TIES ALONG THE TOP OF THE QUILT ALLOW IT TO BE HUNG ON THE WALL FROM THE PEG BOARD. THE FINISHED QUILT CAN BE HAND-WASHED IN LUKEWARM WATER AND DRIED FLAT.

Step 1 Lay the quilt on a flat surface right side up. Spray adhesive on the back of the first stencil and position on the quilt. Rub some oil crayon on a sheet of scrap paper or card and pick up the colour with a stencil brush. Apply the colours individually, using a separate stencil brush for each one. Leave to dry for 24 hours.

Step 2 Finally, attach the ties for hanging the quilt. Work out the position of the tapes across the top edge of the quilt, allowing 15cm/6in gaps between the ties to correspond with the peg board. Cut a length of white tape 30cm/12in long for each tie. Fold in two and pin and stitch to the back of the quilt.

Storage Rack

MOST LARGE WINE STORES SELL PACKS OF SIX BOTTLES OF WINE IN STURDY WOODEN CRATES. WITH A LITTLE RESHAPING, A BOX LIKE THIS CAN BE EASILY TRANSFORMED INTO WALL HANGING STORAGE WHICH IS BOTH PRACTICAL AND BEAUTIFUL IN ITS SIMPLICITY.

Materials and equipment

wooden wine box • brown paper • scissors • pencil • jigsaw • sandpaper • panel pins and hammer • electric drill • acrylic matt varnish or off-white emulsion paint • varnish brush or paintbrush • ribbon

Step 1 Cut a piece of brown paper to match the rectangular back of the box and fold in half lengthwise. Draw a curved line for the top. Cut out and unfold the paper. Place on the back of the box and draw around the curve.

Step 2 Make a second pattern for the sides and transfer it to the box. Remove the top and front of the box, then use a jigsaw to cut along the pencil lines and sand the edges smooth.

Step 3 From the offcuts, saw two 2.5cm/1in wide strips of wood to fit across the front of the box and attach with panel pins. Drill a hole in the centre back.

Step 4 Varnish or paint the box and thread ribbon through the hole with which to hang the box from the peg board.

Stencils

Summer Garden Room

This light, poetical conservatory style

encapsulates the atmosphere of garden rooms

in old French seaside hotels, or tavernas in

Portugal and Spain, where plants, fruit and

flowers are more important to the look than

any work of art. The desire to catch the

freedom of the great outdoors and bring it

inside is every designer's dream. The ultimate

challenge is re-creating the look within

the constraints of the four walls of

an average-sized room.

Focus on Style

Bringing obvious garden elements indoors is the first step to creating this style. Cream, white or pale green walls lined with green or white trellis form an ideal setting. Using trellis to frame a mirror is a good trick to give the room a feeling of open space. To maximize the feeling of space, an all-white room is extremely effective; add a white tiled floor and white furniture so that all the colour comes from green plants, fruit and flowers, which will naturally stand out in contrast.

Masses of plants are vital to the garden atmosphere: if you are not green-fingered you can use artificial ivy to soften the edges of the room. Add to the deception by using scented candles or a room spray to waft a delicious fresh rose smell through the room.

Choose metal in delicate, decorative shapes for planters and chairs, and paint them white so that they do not encroach upon the feeling of space. Avoid solid dark woods which look sturdy and sensible in the garden, but will seem bulky in a small room.

A collection of earthenware pots, either in planters or on shelves around the room, is really all the decoration you need. Fill them with anything that will grow well indoors. Small trees, preferably lemon or orange trees, or even a palm or two, will create a lush, Mediterranean atmosphere.

FLOORS
Earthy shades, like terracotta (real or fake), cork and wood decking for floors are best. If the room happens to open onto a real balcony or patio, cover both floors to match, helping to intergrate indoor and outdoor space.

FABRICS

Fabrics need to evoke the atmosphere of a garden pavilion opening on to a well-manicured lawn. Tenting the ceiling with white voile will suggest the shape created by a sloping glazed roof. White blinds stencilled with garden motifs add a decorative element and evoke a summer atmosphere. Crisp cottons in green and white stripes or leafy prints look fresh and pretty.

ACCESSORIES

Natural materials, such as bamboo, evoke an open-air atmosphere. Use them to make screens or curtain poles. For a crisper look, try green perspex knobs on white painted furniture.

WALLS

Woven rush wallpaper in natural colourways creates a rural garden feel, while introducing texture and continuing the outdoor theme.

Summer Garden Room 67

Tiled Tabletop

C OPY THIS DESIGN OF INTERTWINING ORANGE
BRANCHES TO MAKE A PRETTY BORDER
AROUND PLAIN WHITE TILES. IT'S AN IDEAL
WAY TO RENOVATE A BATTERED TABLETOP, AND IF THE
TILES AREN'T AN EXACT FIT YOU CAN COMPLETE THE
TOP BY GLUING ON STRIPS OF TIMBER OF THE SAME
THICKNESS AS THE TILES. HAND-PAINTED CERAMIC
TILES LOOK EXPENSIVE, BUT THIS DECORATION IS
REMARKABLY EASY TO DO, USING WATER-BASED
CERAMIC PAINTS WHICH CAN BE HARDENED IN A
DOMESTIC OVEN. FOR A FRESH, PROFESSIONAL FINISH,
MINIMIZE THE NUMBER OF COLOURS YOU USE AND
OUTLINE THE SHAPES USING A FELT-TIPPED PEN
SPECIALLY FORMULATED FOR CERAMICS. TO BUILD UP
YOUR CONFIDENCE, TEST THE COLOURS AND BRUSH
STROKES ON A SPARE TILE BEFORE YOU BEGIN.

Materials and equipment

*table • timber battens to frame tabletop • saw and
mitring block • tracing paper or photocopier • pencil •
enough white tiles to cover tabletop • carbon paper •
felt-tipped pens for ceramics in green and red • cotton
wool buds • ceramic paints in olive, emerald green, red
and yellow • medium and fine artist's brushes • old
plate or palette • tile adhesive • wood glue • panel
pins and hammer*

Step 1 Cut four lengths of batten to fit the sides of the tabletop. (The timber should be deep enough to cover the edges of both the table and the tiles.) Mitre the corners to make a frame.

Step 2 Trace or photocopy the leaf and orange pattern on the opposite page and enlarge it to fit your tabletop. Arrange the tiles on the table and transfer the pattern using a sharp pencil and carbon paper.

Step 3 Outline the leaf shapes using the green felt-tipped pen. Draw just outside, not over, the carbon line. Outline the oranges in the same way, using red.

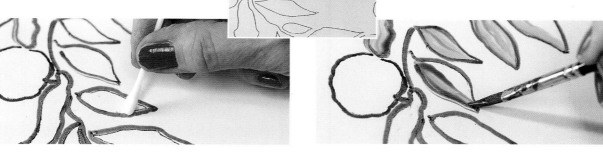

Step 4 Leave to dry for at least 3 hours, then rub off the carbon lines using moistened cotton wool buds.

Step 5 Colour the leaves in olive and emerald green, using two or three long brush strokes for each leaf.

Step 6 Mix red and yellow paint to make orange, and use a medium artist's brush to paint the oranges with a stippling action. Leave to dry.

Step 7 Use the green felt-tipped pen to draw a vein down the centre of each leaf. Harden the paints in the oven following the manufacturer's instructions. When cooled, arrange the tiles on the tabletop and attach using tile adhesive. Finally, glue the timber frame around the tiled area and secure with panel pins.

Trellis Mirror and Flower Vase

A REMARKABLY SIMPLE BUT EFFECTIVE WAY TO CREATE A GARDEN ATMOSPHERE IS TO FURNISH THE ROOM WITH OUTDOOR ELEMENTS LIKE TRELLIS. THE CHARM OF THIS DESIGN IS THE WAY THE FLOWERS ARE REFLECTED IN THE MIRROR, AND THE SENSE OF SPACE IT CREATES. TO BEGIN, POSITION THE MIRROR ON THE WALL, PLACING THE TRELLIS AROUND IT, AND SCREW EVERYTHING IN PLACE.

Materials and equipment

mirror cut to fit within trellis arch, with pre-drilled fixing holes • screws and screwdriver • arched trellis panel • natural raffia • 10 glass test tubes • scissors • 25 x 5mm/1 x ¼in timber batten cut to fit across trellis arch • pencil • 10 metal clips • flowers

Step 1 Wrap a few strands of natural raffia around the top of each test tube. Tie in a knot and trim the ends.

Step 2 Line up the test tubes, evenly spaced, along the wooden batten and mark the positions for the metal clips.

Step 3 Screw the metal clips to the timber batten. Screw the batten to the trellis frame, so that it sits at the foot of the mirror.

Step 4 Clip the test tubes into the metal clips, with the raffia sitting just above the clips. Fill each one with water. Cut all the stems of the flowers to the same length and insert one into each test tube.

Planter Shelf

A PRACTICAL WAY TO SUPPORT PLANT POTS SECURELY ON THE WALL IS BY CUTTING POT-SIZED HOLES IN A WOODEN SHELF. FOR THE BEST VISUAL IMPACT, YOU COULD COVER AN ENTIRE WALL WITH PLANTER SHELVES AND FILL THEM WITH FLOWERING CLIMBERS AND OTHER SPECIES LIKE TRAILING PELARGONIUMS.

**Materials
and equipment**
*small wooden shelf •
2 terracotta pots •
pencil • electric drill
and bit • jigsaw*

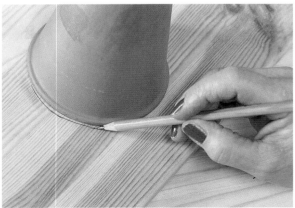

Step 1 Position an upturned pot on the wooden shelf and draw a circle around the shape. Move the pot along the shelf and repeat.

Step 2 Drill a starter hole inside each circle, then use a jigsaw to cut out the shapes, about 5mm/¼in inside the pencil lines so that the pots will not slip through the openings.

Stencilled Blinds

Materials and equipment

photocopier • acetate for stencils • glass sheet or cutting mat masking tape • hot pen or craft knife • white blinds to fit window • spray adhesive • oil stencil crayons in green, yellow, blue, terracotta and red • scrap paper or card • 5 stencil brushes

FOR CITY-DWELLERS WHOSE WINDOWS OVERLOOK A DEPRESSING CONCRETE JUNGLE, IT CAN BE IMPORTANT TO CREATE A SUBSTITUTE VIEW. ACTUAL-SIZE FRUIT TREES, STENCILLED ON TO WHITE BLINDS, LOOK STYLIZED AND ELEGANT. WHEN THE SUN SHINES THROUGH THEM, THEY FILL THE ROOM WITH RUSTIC SHADES OF ORANGE, YELLOW AND GREEN.

Step 1 Photocopy and enlarge lemon and apple tree designs of your choice to fit your blinds, and cut stencils from acetate sheets. Lay each blind flat, right side up. Spray the stencils lightly with adhesive and position on the fabric.

Step 2 Rub some oil crayon on a sheet of scrap paper or card and pick up the colour with a stencil brush. Apply the colours individually, using a separate stencil brush for each one. Leave to dry for 24 hours.

Tuscan Hallway

THE TUSCAN STYLE IS A LEGENDARY ITALIAN MIX

OF INFLUENCES, FROM THE ART AND ARCHITECTURE OF

THE ANCIENT ETRUSCANS AND ROMANS TO THAT

OF THE ITALIAN RENAISSANCE. IT RE-EMERGED AS

THE NEOCLASSICISM IN EUROPE, AND ITS GRAND

ELEGANCE HAS REMAINED POPULAR EVER SINCE.

FULL OF WARM OPULENCE, IT IS A DECORATING

SCHEME GUARANTEED TO MAKE A HALL OR DINING

ROOM LOOK STRIKINGLY SUMPTUOUS.

Focus on Style

Even without the help of authentic architectural proportions, grand arches and pillars, it is still possible to achieve this look just by choosing the right combination of textures, colours and furniture. Try a terracotta colourwash for walls, a stencilled mosaic floor, a distressed gilded mirror, silk swags and wall sconces. Add a few pieces of timeless unglazed pottery and some distinguished-looking medieval-style furniture. Create 'hot' light by filtering it through fretted shutters and the sum total will translate into a welcoming hallway full of Mediterranean warmth.

Mosaic borders or whole mosaic panels can be created with stencils, applied with a small roller for a chipped, patchy, aged appearance. Mosaic – real or painted – is also ideal for the floor, as are ceramics, slate or marble. If you are using tiles, the larger they are the more historically authentic they will look, so avoid the smaller modern standard sizes.

Because Roman textile remains are so rare, their appearance has been largely reinvented by informed designers. Drawing inspiration from ancient painted vases and frescoes, it can be assumed that plain colours and simple classical imagery were the fashion of the day.

WALLS
Colourwashing is the ideal paint effect, or you could apply filler with a flat trowel to emulate the texture of old plaster and finish with a coat of diluted emulsion paint. Shades of sun-baked earth in faded terracotta and ochre, mixed with the bleached pink and ivory found on old plastered walls and in Italian frescos, are the colours to aim for.

FURNITURE

Distressed textures can be easily achieved using a base coat of terracotta, black or deep blue (often used to paint the Madonna's robes in Renaissance paintings) with a top coat of Dutch metal which resembles gold leaf. Rub back the gilding to reveal patches of colour below.

FABRICS

Swagged silks and damasks, with metallic threads simulating gold and silver, create regal plushness in keeping with what is essentially a luxurious look.

FLOORS

Ceramic or mosaic floors are vital to this look. You can buy intricately patterned mosaic flooring pre-laid on large tiles, which are expensive but capture the idea perfectly.

ACCESSORIES

Gold or black door handles and curtain finials suit this style. Greek key borders, half urns, scroll and lyre designs can all be used to decorate frames and furniture.

Console Table

O F ALL THE DECORATIVE EFFECTS USED TO AGE FURNITURE, LAYERING WITH PAINT IS ONE OF THE SIMPLEST AND MOST TRADITIONAL. DILUTE BLACK EMULSION PAINT, COVERED BY A LAYER OF DEEP TURQUOISE, CLEVERLY RE-CREATES THE PATINA OF AGE ACCUMULATED OVER CENTURIES. TWO NARROW LINES OF GILDING HAVE BEEN USED TO ENHANCE THE SEMI-CIRCULAR SHAPE OF THE TABLE. A ROW OF CARVED MEDALLIONS ADDS THE FINAL TOUCH. THESE ARE SOLD AS PELMET PIN-HOLDERS AND CAN BE BOUGHT READY-GILDED.

Materials and equipment

MDF console table • matt emulsion paint in turquoise and black • decorator's paintbrush and small artist's brush • sandpaper • acrylic scumble glaze • paint kettle • flexible masking tape • acrylic gold size • gold Dutch metal leaf • acrylic varnish • varnish brush • 7 small carved medallions • wood glue

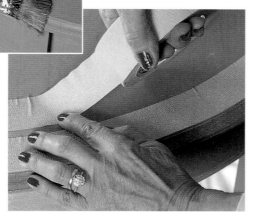

Step 1 Paint the table with two coats of turquoise paint, sanding between coats. Mix a glaze using one part scumble to two parts black emulsion paint and apply in random strokes all over the table to age it. Leave to dry.

Step 2 Dilute the turquoise paint with a little water, and paint over the black glaze to soften the effect. Mask a line around the top edge of the table using flexible masking tape.

Step 3 Using a small artist's brush, apply gold size to the masked line and leave until it feels tacky (about 10 minutes). Apply a leaf of Dutch metal to the gold size and rub the backing paper thoroughly. Run your fingernail along the edges to ensure a clean line.

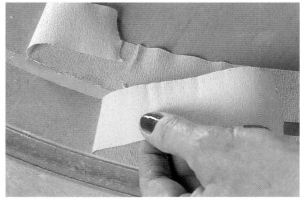

Step 4 Lift the backing paper away from the Dutch metal leaf. Continue around the masked line then leave for 24 hours to settle.

Step 5 Remove the masking tape and repeat the process to gild the moulded edge of the table. Finish with two coats of acrylic varnish. Glue the gold medallions, equally spaced, around the side of the table.

Gilded Mirror Frame

THE WORLD IS FULL OF PLAIN PICTURE FRAMES WHICH, SKILFULLY PAINTED AND GILDED, CAN BE MADE TO LOOK LIKE ANTIQUES. ON THIS MIRROR FRAME, THE TOP SURFACE OF TURQUOISE PAINT WAS RUBBED BACK TO REVEAL PATCHES OF THE TERRACOTTA BASE COAT. THE MIDDLE SECTION WAS GILDED USING DUTCH METAL. CARVED WOODEN ORNAMENTS WERE USED TO DECORATE EACH CORNER.

Materials and equipment

mirror in moulded frame • matt emulsion paint in terracotta and turquoise • decorator's paintbrush • sandpaper • masking tape • acrylic gold size • gold Dutch metal leaf • 4 carved wooden ornaments • wood glue • acrylic matt varnish • varnish brush

Step 1 Take the mirror out of its frame. Paint the frame with a base coat of terracotta emulsion paint and leave to dry. Apply a second coat of turquoise emulsion paint. When dry, sand the edges of the mirror to allow the base coat to show through.

Step 2 Mask the frame around the flat central recess. Cover the recess with gold size and leave until it feels tacky (about 10 minutes).

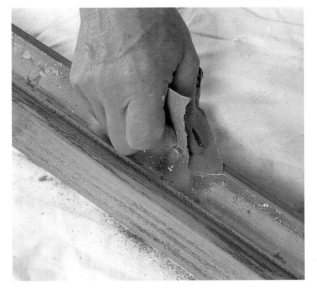

Step 3 Apply the Dutch metal leaf and smooth it on to the tacky surface using a dry brush, then lift off the backing paper. Do not worry if the Dutch metal leaves some broken edges as this will add to the mellow, aged look. Leave the gilding to settle for 24 hours.

Step 4 Rub back the metal leaf in places to reveal the colour beneath. Gild the carved corner decorations using the same process and glue in place. Protect the frame with acrylic varnish.

Amaryllis Topiary Tree

FOR A FORMAL AND STRIKING ARRANGEMENT OF EXOTIC LILIES, THIS 'TOPIARY TREE' IS AN IDEAL ARRANGEMENT TO PLACE ON A DEEP WINDOWSILL. YOU NEED ONLY A FEW LARGE FLOWER HEADS TO MAKE A BIG IMPACT. LILIES ARE OFTEN DEPICTED IN RENAISSANCE PAINTINGS HELD BY THE MADONNA OR ANGELIC FIGURES SO THEY ARE TRULY APPROPRIATE TO THE STYLE.

Materials and equipment
flower arranger's spiked metal stem-holder • flat, wide glass bowl • 7 amaryllis stems • scissors • 2 elastic bands or garden string • pebbles

Step 1 Place the stem-holder in the middle of the bowl. Cut all the amaryllis stems to the same length. Hold the heads together with an elastic band or garden string positioned just below the petals. Place the second elastic band around the cut ends of the stems.

Step 2 Position the 'tree' upright in the dish by carefully pushing the stems into the stem-holder. Conceal the support with pebbles and fill the dish with water.

Mosaic Wall Stencil

Step 1 Decide on the height of the top of the border and mark all four walls using a pencil, straight edge and spirit level. Stretch a length of string across each wall at this height to act as a guideline.

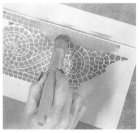

Step 2 Photocopy and enlarge the border design on page 85, and cut from acetate. Spray the back of the stencil lightly with adhesive and place it along the marked line. Apply each colour with a separate brush.

Step 3 To create a patchy, antique effect, make sure that the colours overlap in places. Use the deep jade to accentuate the outside border edges.

Materials and equipment

pencil and straight edge • spirit level • string • drawing pins • acetate for stencil • glass sheet or cutting mat • masking tape • hot pen or craft knife • spray adhesive • matt emulsion paints in deep jade, aqua, burgundy and yellow ochre • 4 stencil brushes • paper towel

WHEN APPLIED TO A WARM TERRACOTTA COLOURWASHED WALL, A WIDE BAND OF STENCILLING CREATES A SUGGESTION OF INLAID MOSAIC, ADDING A PATCHWORK OF JEWEL-LIKE COLOURS AT DADO HEIGHT.

Stencilled Mosaic Floor

Materials and equipment

vinyl silk emulsion paint in sand, aqua, dark green and off-white • large decorator's paintbrush • string • 4 drawing pins • pencil and straight edge • acetate for stencils • glass sheet or cutting mat • masking tape • hot pen or craft knife • spray adhesive • small paint roller and tray • paper towels • floor varnish • varnish brush

T HE PAINT FOR THIS FLOOR WAS APPLIED WITH A SMALL ROLLER TO GIVE A PATCHY, WELL-WORN EFFECT AT A FRACTION OF THE COST AND WEIGHT OF REAL MOSAIC. THE PRICELESS-LOOKING RESULT IS REMINISCENT OF 16TH-CENTURY FLORENTINE FLOORS. THE SAND-COLOURED BASE COAT IS PROBABLY CLOSEST TO THE COLOUR OF THE MORTAR THAT WOULD HAVE BEEN USED TO CEMENT REAL MOSAIC, LABORIOUSLY LAID BY HAND. THE MORE COATS OF PROTECTIVE FLOOR VARNISH YOU HAVE THE PATIENCE TO APPLY, THE BETTER THE FLOOR WILL WEAR.

Step 1 Paint the floor with two coats of sand-coloured vinyl silk emulsion paint and leave to dry. Find the centre of the floor using two long pieces of string, fixed across the diagonals of the room with drawing pins. Mark the point where they cross. Using a pencil and straight edge, draw a line around the edge of the room, 10cm/4in from the skirting board.

Step 2 Photocopy and enlarge the mosaic tile and border stencils opposite, and cut out of acetate. Spray the border stencil lightly with adhesive and position it along the line. Stencil in dark green paint using a small roller. To make sure the roller is not overloaded, roll it over paper towels before applying it to the stencil. Repeat the border design all round the room.

Step 3 Starting from the centre of the room, place the tile stencil parallel with the border and stencil using aqua emulsion paint and the small roller. Alternate the colours to create a turquoise and off-white mosaic tile effect. When you reach the border, you will probably need to mask the stencil to fit it in. Protect the floor with several coats of varnish.

Stencils

Victorian Bathroom

Despite the overbearing and sombre aspect
of much Victorian style, it has some positive
characteristics – a sense of comfort, integrity
and luxury – which continues to appeal.
The Victorians were great engineers and
invented the bathroom as we know it. Their
ornate and sturdy sanitary ware is still the
envy of the world, and modern copies of
Victorian bathroom suites remain popular.
If your bathroom is big enough, this is
a style worth emulating.

Focus on Style

In search of a modern interpretation of what was originally a very fussy style, this bathroom incorporates panelling instead of tiles, which can be visually rather busy. Stained, leaded and etched windows were inherent to Victorian architecture but today's versatile craft products can transform modern windows to resemble the originals.

Walls were often covered in strongly patterned wallpaper, and there was a great fashion for closely hung prints and watercolours. Black and white floor tiles or dark-mahogany stained floorboards were typical. For today's rooms, some Victorian-style wallpapers and soft colours like terracotta, red, blue-grey and green are warm, relaxed shades, compatible with most pale modern furniture.

WALLS
Rich colours and strong patterns evoke the Victorian style on modern walls. If actual reproductions are too sombre or over-powering, choose colours in a softer shade.

Mahogany was a Victorian favourite. Washstands and side tables sometimes had marble tops; chairs were upholstered in velvet, damask and leather. Except in kitchens, painted furniture was not the norm. Despite this, battered junk-shop finds can still make good shapes for transformations, but combine painted finishes with découpage using flower prints or calligraphy, and add marble or glass tops.

Damask, velvet, lace and silk curtains were finished with heavy tassels and trimmings. Fabric was used profusely for pelmets and tablecloths as well as throws and curtains. No Victorian-style room would be complete without a surfeit of *objets*: perhaps a pair of china dogs, some silhouette miniatures or a collection of framed prints. Flat figures cut from plywood, like the bathers on the previous page, are examples of the humorous side of late Victorian decoration.

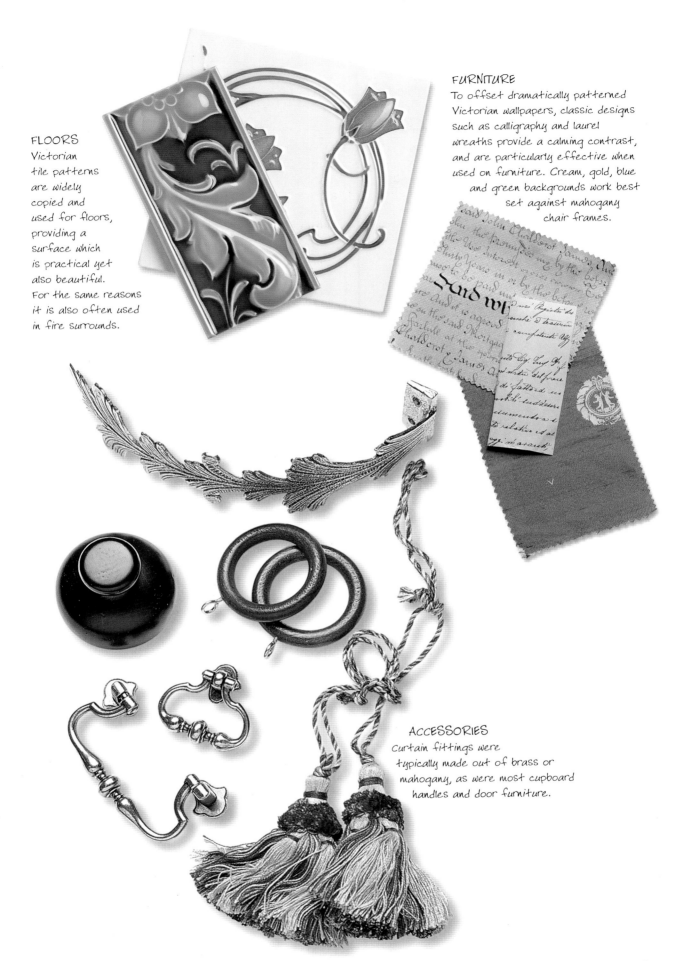

FLOORS
Victorian tile patterns are widely copied and used for floors, providing a surface which is practical yet also beautiful. For the same reasons it is also often used in fire surrounds.

FURNITURE
To offset dramatically patterned Victorian wallpapers, classic designs such as calligraphy and laurel wreaths provide a calming contrast, and are particularly effective when used on furniture. Cream, gold, blue and green backgrounds work best set against mahogany chair frames.

ACCESSORIES
Curtain fittings were typically made out of brass or mahogany, as were most cupboard handles and door furniture.

Decoupage Bathroom Cupboard

Materials and equipment

small cupboard with glass top • off-white emulsion paint • decorator's paintbrush • collection of wine labels • plain paper • spray adhesive • screwdriver • wallpaper paste • dry cloth • script-printed paper • scissors • tinted acrylic varnish • varnish brush • 2 cupboard-door handles

T HE ART OF DECORATING SURFACES BY APPLYING PAPER CUT-OUTS PROTECTED WITH VARNISH WAS A FAVOURITE VICTORIAN PASTIME, USED TO CREATE THE LOOK OF HAND-PAINTED FURNITURE. WINE LABELS ARE PARTICULARLY SUITED TO DECOUPAGE, ESPECIALLY THE *PREMIER CRU* LABELS, WHICH ARE FAMOUS FOR THEIR DECORATIVE QUALITIES AND OFTEN INCORPORATE A LINE DRAWING OF THE CHATEAU OR VINEYARD. SOAK THE BOTTLES IN WATER TO EASE OFF THE LABELS AND DRY THEM FLAT ON A SOFT CLOTH. YOU NEED ONLY COLLECT A FEW LABELS AND THEN PHOTOCOPY THEM UNTIL YOU HAVE THE RIGHT AMOUNT (SEE STEP 1). AS AN ALTERNATIVE TO ACRYLIC VARNISH YOU COULD USE A CRACKLE VARNISH TO INCREASE THE AGED EFFECT.

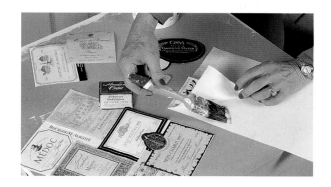

Step 1 Paint the parts of the cupboard that will not be covered in découpage with two coats of off-white emulsion paint, sanding between coats. Leave to dry. Arrange the wine labels, edge to edge, on a sheet of plain paper and glue in place using spray adhesive. Take the sheet to your local photocopier for as many colour copies as you need to cover the cupboard.

Step 2 Remove the cupboard hinges. Mix the wallpaper paste, following the manufacturer's instructions, and paste the labels over the cupboard doors and sides. Smooth with a cloth to avoid bubbling.

Step 3 Cut the script paper to fit the top of the cupboard and glue in place.

Step 4 Leave for 24 hours to dry, then apply two coats of tinted acrylic varnish. Replace the cupboard doors and glass top, and attach the door handles.

Etched Glass Window

Materials and equipment

ruler and wax pencil • self-adhesive lead tape • scissors • bone folder • blue self-adhesive transparent plastic sheet • craft knife • acetate for stencils • glass sheet or cutting mat • masking tape • hot pen (optional) • spray adhesive • scrap paper or card • glass etching spray

Victorian architecture often incorporated designs for stained and etched glass windows. These days, so many urban windows overlook dismal exteriors that this window treatment is worth considering even if you do not want a Victorian look: just give it an alternative style using different stencils.

Step 1 Measure 12.5cm/5in in from the window frame and rule a border all round the window using a wax pencil. The lines should cross to form a square in each corner of the window.

Step 2 Carefully peel the backing paper from the self-adhesive lead tape and stick in place, using the lines as a guide and cutting with scissors where necessary. Smooth down firmly with a bone folder.

Step 3 Roughly cut the coloured plastic sheet to fit the border sections. Peel away the backing paper and smooth the sheets on to the glass.

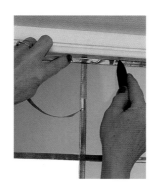

Step 4 Cut away any excess plastic using a craft knife.

Step 5 Apply a length of lead tape around the outside of the border, next to the window frame.

Step 6 Photocopy and enlarge the wreath and appropriate initial stencils on pages 96–7, and cut out of acetate. Spray the back of the wreath stencil with adhesive and centre it on the window pane. Mask around the stencil with sheets of paper or card. Spray the stencil with glass etching spray, following the manufacturer's instructions. Repeat for the stencilled initials.

Silk Wall Banner

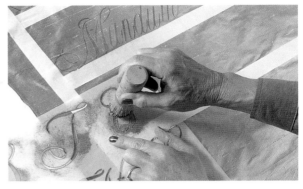

Step 1 Cut the silk to the width and length required, allowing an extra 10cm/4in at the top. Fold, pin and stitch a channel at the top of the banner to fit over the curtain pole. Photocopy the alphabet stencils on page 97 and cut them out of acetate.

Step 2 Plan the layout of the inscription, spacing the lines of text evenly. Mark their positions with tailor's chalk, then use masking tape to form clear guidelines for the stencils. Spray the back of each letter stencil with spray adhesive and stencil the letters using gilt cream and a stencil brush.

Step 3 Light a candle and hold it to the raw edge of the silk until the fabric begins to curl. It should burn out by itself, but have a damp cloth ready to prevent accidents. Singe the sides and bottom of the banner, and thread on to the pole.

THIS BANNER CONTINUES THE CALLIGRAPHIC THEME, AND IS INSCRIBED WITH UPLIFTING BIBLICAL TEXT. USE THE ALPHABET ON PAGE 97 TO PLAN THE TEXT OF YOUR CHOICE.

Materials and equipment

length of plain raw silk fabric • scissors • pins • sewing machine and matching thread • acetate for stencils • glass sheet or cutting mat • masking tape • hot pen or craft knife • ruler • tailor's chalk • spray adhesive • gilt cream • stencil brush • candle and matches • damp cloth • curtain pole and fittings

Silhouette Miniatures

Step 1 Photograph your subjects in profile in front of a plain, contrasting background. When the film is developed, trace around the outline of each head.

Step 2 Carefully fill in the shapes with a black felt-tipped pen. Make photocopies of your silhouettes.

Step 3 Cut each silhouette into an oval shape and fit into a miniature frame, taking care not to bend any of the features.

A CHARMING WAY TO CAPTURE THE LIKENESSES OF CHILDREN AND OTHER LOVED ONES, SILHOUETTE-CUTTING WAS POPULAR WITH THE VICTORIANS. MANY YOUNG LADIES LEARNED TO SNIP MINIATURE PORTRAITS OUT OF BLACK PAPER, AND PRACTICALLY EVERY FAMILY HAD A COLLECTION OF SILHOUETTES. THIS IS A QUICK AND EASY WAY TO ACHIEVE A SIMILAR EFFECT.

Materials and equipment

camera • tracing paper • pencil • black felt-tipped pen • scissors • black Victorian-style miniature frames

Stencils

A B C D E
F G H I J
K L M N
O P Q R S
T U V W X
Y Z

a b c d e f g h i j k l m n o p
q r s t u v w x y z

Romantic
Parisian
Bedroom

Traditionally the world's most romantic city,

Paris takes first place in the romantic

boudoir style stakes, although the look has

been reinterpreted worldwide and through

all generations. Silky, sophisticated and

seductive, the style combines French chic

with a hint of Hollywood glitz. Elegant

opulence and comfort are key ingredients.

Focus on Style

The romantic look is full of floating fabrics, soft, sensual textures and glittering surfaces. Delicately shaped furniture and mirrored accessories blend with wild silk and glittering gauzes, crisp white linen, scented candles, exotic flowers and a deep pile carpet. A pattern of leaves trails over the walls and the leafy silk canopy suggests both intimacy and a sense of ceremony. Translucent textures and mirrored mosaic surfaces add the necessary sparkle.

On the floor, nothing beats the luxury of a deep-pile off-white fitted carpet. So despite the current fashion for bare boards and sisal, this look demands good quality carpet. If your room has a wooden floor that is too good to hide, choose a large silky Chinese-style rug to soften it.

Organza voile shot with metal threads is perfectly suited to this look. Like wire-edged ribbons, wire-threaded fabrics can be sculpted to hang in extravagant folds. Voiles spattered with mirror beads can be softly draped over a curtain pole.

To create the right seductive atmosphere, soft lighting – preferably from recessed halogen spots linked to a dimmer – is worth the investment. An exotic fresh flower arrangement, some silver-backed brushes and delicate cut-glass scent bottles will accentuate the feminine feel.

WALLS
Plain and metallic pastels in creamy yellow, pale lilac, pink, and blue grey are ideally calm colours to marry up with accents in gold and silver.

ACCESSORIES

For accessories in the room, deep bluish-purple, silver and rich terracotta are traditionally opulent colours which you could juxtapose in a collection of glass, pots or vases.

FABRICS

Raw silk stencilled with silver leaves, metallic lace and other sumptuous silks and damasks in white and pale pastels will inject the necessary glamour.

ACCESSORIES

Silver tassels and fringing, glass beads, heart-shaped hooks and sparkling mirrors provide romantic finishing touches.

Romantic Parisian Bedroom 101

Antique-style Dressing Table

WHITE AND GOLD ARE A WELL-TESTED DUO IN THE GLAMOUR STAKES. PAINTING THE PIECE FIRST IN A SAFFRON COLOUR WILL SAVE MONEY ON GOLD PAINT, WHICH TENDS TO BE EXPENSIVE. OVER THE GOLD BASE, THE WHITE IS PATCHILY APPLIED TO CREATE A SOFT PATINA. TURNED DETAILS ON THE LEGS HAVE BEEN ACCENTUATED BY APPLYING A THINNER COAT OF OFF-WHITE PAINT.

Materials and equipment

MDF table • matt emulsion paint in saffron yellow and off-white • household paintbrush • sandpaper • gold acrylic paint • 1cm/½in wide masking tape • small paint roller and tray • paper towels • PVA glue

Step 1 Paint the entire table in saffron yellow emulsion paint. Leave to dry, then sand smooth and paint a second coat in gold paint.

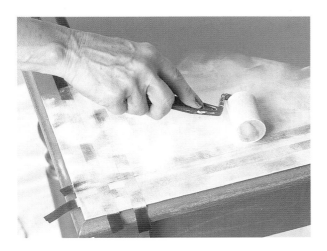

Step 2 When the paint is dry, apply strips of masking tape all round the tabletop, about 2.5cm/1in from the outside edge. Apply a second set of strips, parallel with the first, leaving about 1cm/½in between the two lines of tape. Dip a small paint roller in off-white emulsion, wipe off the excess on paper towels and roll over the top of the table, working in all directions to create an antique, patchy effect. The paint must not look translucent but the covering should not be solid. Paint the sides, front and back, leaving the table edge gold.

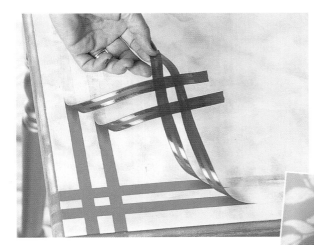

Step 3 Remove the masking tape. Mask the turned tops and bottoms of the table legs and run the roller, loaded with off-white emulsion, over the legs. Leave to dry, then remove the masking tape and apply a coat of dilute emulsion to the remaining, turned, parts of the legs. When dry, protect the table with a coat of PVA glue, which will give a rich beeswax effect.

Mosaic Mirror

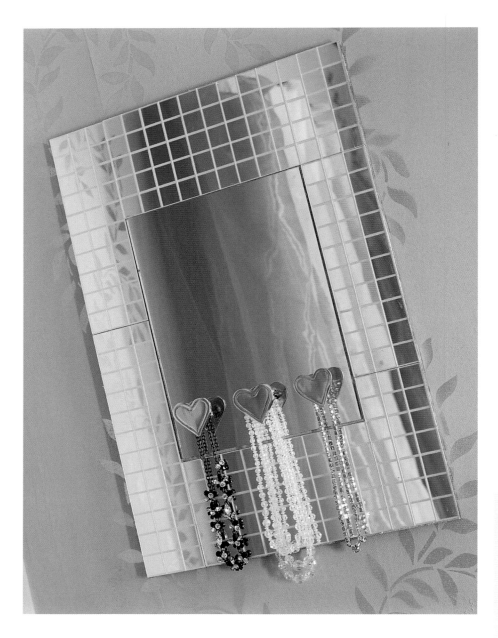

Materials and equipment
23 x 30cm/9 x 12in mirror • 38 x 56cm/ 15 x 22in piece of 1cm/½in MDF • ruler and pencil • masking tape • electric drill with masonry bit • 3 sheets mirror mosaic • craft knife • tile adhesive • 3 heart-shaped door knobs • picture wire • picture hook • hammer

MIRROR MOSAICS CAN BE BOUGHT READY-MOUNTED ON A FABRIC BACKING, WITH A CLEVER EDGING THAT SIMULATES REAL GROUTING. THEY MAKE THIS PROJECT INCREDIBLY QUICK TO UNDERTAKE. IF YOU ARE NERVOUS ABOUT DRILLING GLASS, ASK THE GLAZIER TO PRE-DRILL THE HOLES FOR THE HEART-SHAPED HOOKS WHEN YOU BUY THE MIRROR.

Step 1 Position the mirror in the centre of the MDF board and draw around it. Mark three equally spaced holes along the bottom of the mirror. To stop the drill bit from skating over the surface, mask the holes with masking tape. Drill three holes to take the knobs.

Step 2 Centre the mirror on the board again and mark the positions for the knobs on the wood. Drill three holes to take the screws.

Step 3 Glue the mirror in place on the backing board. Cut the mosaic sheets to fit around the central mirror by scoring through the fabric backing.

Step 4 Glue the mosaic panels in place to create a frame.

Step 5 Screw the door knobs in place on the mirror. Screw two picture eyelet screws into the back of the frame and thread picture wire between them. Hang on a picture hook.

Stencilled Walls

Step 1 Enlarge the symmetrical leaf design on pages 108–109 and cut the stencil from acetate. Calculate how the stencil pattern will fit within the width of each wall. Pin a plumb line to the top of the first wall. Spray the back of the stencil with adhesive and position on the wall.

Step 2 Following the paint manufacturer's instructions, spray through the stencil on to the wall, masking the edges with paper or card.

Step 3 Peel off the stencil and reposition. Repeat the process until the walls are covered.

U SING A LARGE FLOWING LEAF STENCIL AND SILVER SPRAY, IT IS QUICKER AND CHEAPER TO STENCIL WALLS THAN TO APPLY WALLPAPER. THE LILAC BASE COMBINED WITH SILVER CREATES A DECIDEDLY GLAMOROUS FEEL. LIKE ANY REFLECTIVE SURFACE, THE SILVER ENHANCES THE FEELING OF LIGHT AND SPACE. USE SILVER-GILT CREAM APPLIED WITH A STENCIL BRUSH TO STENCIL A SILK CANOPY TO MATCH.

Materials and equipment

acetate for stencil • glass sheet or cutting mat • masking tape • hot pen or craft knife • tape measure • pencil • plumb line • spray adhesive • silver spray paint • scrap paper or card

Flower Arrangement

Materials and equipment
*large fan palm leaf •
scissors • exotic lily •
narrow-necked vase*

Step 1 With the closed tips of a pair of scissors, make a hole in the leaf near the stem.

Step 2 Cut the flower stem to the same length as the leaf stem and thread through the hole in the leaf. Insert both stems in the vase.

N O ROMANTIC BEDROOM WOULD BE COMPLETE WITHOUT A STYLISH FLORAL ARRANGEMENT. IF YOU MAKE HOLES IN A LARGE LEAF, IT WILL ACT AS A SUPPORT FOR THE FLOWERS, CUPPING AND HOLDING THE HEADS JUST WHERE YOU WANT THEM. SMALL FLOWER HEADS CAN BE ARRANGED IN A HEART SHAPE, PROVIDING THE LEAF IS LARGE ENOUGH.

Stencils

French Rural Kitchen

Representing an unchanging lifestyle where

jam is home-made and time counts for little,

the French farmhouse style is an ideal look

for a large kitchen. It is sturdy, countrified,

comfortable and cosily old-fashioned.

The atmosphere is well lived-in, relaxed

and faintly ramshackle.

Focus on Style

Aspects of French domestic architecture – thick plastered walls, high ceilings and panelled shutters – play a vital role in creating this look. Rough textures, like the flagstone floor, and sun-faded colours are important ingredients. Walls should be colourwashed, painted or wood-panelled. The texture of old plaster can be simulated with modern imitations, like the impasto finish used on the armoire on page 114.

Farmhouse floors are subject to muddy boots and even a stray chicken or two, so they need to be hard-wearing and practical. Large robust flagstones or well-worn terracotta tiles will reinforce a link with the outdoor life and may even match a courtyard outside.

Solidly built free-standing units, like a large armoire, butcher's block and ceramic sink, are important. Furniture should be convincingly distressed. For curtains, red and white gingham may be a visual cliché but it sums up the French farmhouse look. However, shutters are still the most traditional choice of window treatment.

Open shelves filled with cooking pots and hand-thrown and painted china decorate the walls. Strings of garlic and stacks of wicker baskets filled with vegetables, and maybe even logs for the fire, will reinforce the ramshackle country look. A large, well-stocked wine rack completes the look.

WALLS
Period paint colours such as dusty ochre, duck-egg blue, French grey and drab green are well documented in the French farmhouse tradition.

FLOORS
A terracotta floor with a tiled pattern border, or a smooth tile in dark grey or honey beige make good alternatives to traditional flagstones, especially in a small kitchen where the scale of large flagstones would be overpowering.

ACCESSORIES
Hammered metal handles and hinges look effective on cupboard doors and shutters.

FABRICS
Woven cottons in classic crisp stripes, checks and simple prints are great for tablecloths and café-style curtains.

French Rural Kitchen 113

French Armoire

REAL ANTIQUE VERSIONS OF THIS IMPOSING PIECE OF FURNITURE ARE MUCH SOUGHT-AFTER AND CORRESPONDINGLY EXPENSIVE. USING IMPASTO PLASTER IS A CLEVER METHOD OF CREATING TEXTURE ON A FLAT MDF BASE AND THE RAISED STENCIL IS A SIMPLE WAY TO IMITATE WOODCARVING. RUBBING BACK THE TOP COAT OF PAINT WILL REVEAL THE PLASTER BELOW, TO GIVE THE PIECE A SUITABLY WELL-WORN AIR.

Materials and equipment
MDF armoire • impasto plaster • medium decorator's paintbrush • stippling brush • plasterer's trowel • acetate for stencil • glass sheet or cutting mat • masking tape • hot pen or craft knife • spray adhesive • French filling knife • matt emulsion paint in buff and apricot • medium-grade sandpaper • matt acrylic varnish • varnish brush • 6 metal handles

Step 1 Mix the impasto plaster, following the manufacturer's directions. Apply the first coat with a decorator's brush.

Step 2 While the plaster is still wet, stipple the surface to create a rough texture.

Step 3 Apply a second coat using a trowel to create a rough plaster effect and leave to dry for 2–4 hours. Copy and enlarge the three-leaf design on page 121 and cut a stencil from acetate sheet.

Step 4 Spray the back of the stencil with adhesive and place in the middle of each cupboard door and drawer front in turn. Relief-stencil the shape using the impasto plaster as a filler and applying it with a French filling knife. Carefully remove the stencil and leave to dry.

Step 5 Apply a coat of buff emulsion paint. When this is dry, apply the apricot emulsion in patches only.

Step 6 Using sandpaper, rub back all the surfaces to reveal some of the white plaster below. Finish with a protective coat of matt acrylic varnish and screw the handles on to the doors and drawers.

Window Shutters

M ADE TO A TRADITIONAL FRENCH DESIGN, THESE SHUTTERS CAN BE PURELY DECORATIVE, BUT IF
YOU WANT TO CLOSE THEM OVER THE WINDOW, REPEAT THE SUPERIMPOSED MDF SHAPE ON BOTH
SIDES AND USE HINGES TO SECURE THEM TO A FRAME AROUND THE WINDOW. TO SIMULATE REAL
WOOD-GRAIN, A GRAINER ROCKED AND DRAGGED THROUGH THICKENED GLAZE IS AMAZINGLY EFFECTIVE.

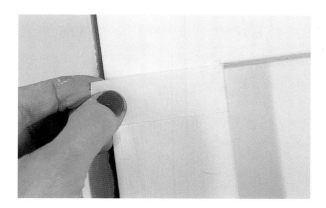

Step 1 Using the picture on the opposite page as a guide, draw the shutter design on each piece of MDF, with the help of a ruler and a pair of compasses. Cut out with a jigsaw. Attach the plywood with panel pins to make a backing. Seal the wood with a coat of PVA glue and, when dry, paint with two coats of off-white emulsion. Mask the top edges of the shutters to make a horizontal 'plank'.

Step 2 Make up a glaze by mixing wallpaper paste with yellow ochre emulsion paint to the consistency of thick porridge. Apply to the top horizontal 'plank'.

Step 3 Work along the area with the wood-grainer, rocking it gently.

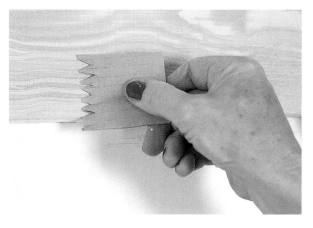

Step 4 Draw the serrated cardboard comb through the glaze to make a plain striped texture to either side of the wood-grained area. Repeat the process to paint a wood-grain effect over the rest of each shutter, working 'planks' where needed. Protect with several coats of acrylic varnish.

French Rural Kitchen 117

Painted Plates

H AND-PAINTED POTTERY IS ONE OF THE
MOST POPULAR CRAFTS IN ANY RURAL
CULTURE AND IN FRANCE THERE ARE MANY
TRADITIONAL DESIGNS TO COPY. OLIVES AND CHERRIES
ARE POSSIBLY THE EASIEST SHAPES TO START WITH.
WATER-BASED CERAMIC PAINTS CAN BE FIRED IN A
DOMESTIC OVEN TO HARDEN THEM.

Materials and equipment

*pencil and paper • carbon paper • plain white plates •
water-based ceramic paints in light brown, mid green,
dark green, bright red, dark red, lilac, dark purple • fine
and medium artist's brushes • palette or old plate •
household sponge*

Step 1 Copy the cherry and/or olive designs on the opposite page, enlarging as necessary, and transfer them to plates using carbon paper.

Step 2 Begin by painting the cherry stalks light brown using a fine brush, painting from the top of the stalk to the cherry in one stroke.

Step 3 Using mid green and a medium brush, paint the cherry leaves in two strokes, one on either side of each leaf. Add a dark green outline to each leaf using a fine brush. For the olive leaves, paint a single outline in mid green but elongating the shape.

Step 4 Using bright red and a medium brush, paint the cherries in two semi-circular strokes, starting at the top, leaving a small sliver of white in between. Add a short stroke to one side of each cherry in dark red. With a medium brush, paint the olives, creating a more elongated olive shape, making one side of each lilac, and the other dark purple.

Step 5 To create the border, dilute green paint with a little water and dip a damp sponge into it. Holding the sponge against the edge, rotate the plate towards you. Harden the paints in the oven following the manufacturer's instructions.

Plate Rack

THERE IS NOW SUCH A GOOD RANGE OF READY-FRETTED DECORATIVE MDF STRIPS TO CHOOSE FROM THAT THIS PROJECT IS IDEAL FOR AMATEUR CARPENTERS. OBVIOUSLY THE LENGTH OF THE RACK CAN BE ADAPTED TO SUIT YOUR WALL SPACE. FOR MAXIMUM EFFECT, COVER A WHOLE WALL WITH A LARGE COLLECTION. BY SCREWING CUP HOOKS TO THE BASE YOU COULD DISPLAY CUPS OR MUGS AS WELL AS PLATES.

Step 2 Drill a line of holes through the narrow side of the timber, about 25cm/10in apart. Using a spirit level, place the wood against the wall and use a pencil to mark the position of the holes. Drill and plug the wall, then attach the shelf.

Materials and equipment
5 x 2.5cm/2 x 1in planed timber • MDF fretwork trim • saw • electric drill • spirit level • pencil • wall plugs • screws and screwdriver • wood glue • panel pins and hammer

Step 1 Cut the timber and fretwork trim to the required length of the plate rack.

Step 3 Place the MDF trim over the wood so that it forms a lip high enough to support the plates. Attach to the shelf with wood glue, reinforced with a line of panel pins.

Stencil

Japanese Dining Room

ANYONE WHO HAS EVER STUDIED INTERIORS IN

JAPAN CANNOT HELP BUT BE IMPRESSED BY THE

SENSE OF DISCIPLINE THAT CHARACTERIZES THESE

UNCLUTTERED SPACES. JAPANESE DESIGNERS EXCEL

IN THE ART OF ONE-ROOM LIVING BASED ON

CENTURIES OF CULTURAL NECESSITY, AND THE

RESULT HAS BEEN THE HIGHLY SUCCESSFUL QUEST

FOR SIMPLICITY AND SERENITY. THIS DINING ROOM

SCHEME ATTEMPTS TO CAPTURE THAT FEELING,

DOING SO WITH A TINTED PALETTE, NATURAL

MATERIALS AND CLEAN LINES.

Focus on Style

The most popular Japanese colour scheme is parchment and red, with accents in black, gold or silver. These vibrant ingredients can form the basis of an opulent dining room, hallway or small cloakroom. Most western pale beech and pine furniture will happily mix with bamboo and red and black lacquer, while in the East, western seating has now superseded floor cushions, which has made the style even easier to adopt. Black, moss-green, gold and silver are traditional accent colours. For an antique effect, apply a black glaze with a dragging brush over a gold base.

Sliding screens or shutters are not difficult to incorporate into modern rooms, and the strong visual rhythm of room dividers, so characteristic of Japanese interiors, is easily simulated with vertical moulding, painted black and fastened to walls at equal intervals. For a striking Japanese accent in a room scheme, stencil calligraphy on to furniture and walls. Traditional scrolls and kimonos, with a bamboo pole slotted through the sleeves, make wonderful wall decorations.

Other authentic finishing touches include futons, rice bowls and chopsticks, lacquered textures, wicker furniture, polished pebbles, a simple arrangement of orchids and bamboo, and even driftwood.

WALLS AND FURNITURE
Bamboo furniture is easy to come by; traditional black and red lacquered pieces are not so easy. Fortunately, on modern materials like MDF it is possible to emulate the smooth, glossy finish using red or black emulsion paint and a high-gloss acrylic varnish. In a small room, red – which can be bright, deep or a dull antique shade – used on walls and ceilings will create a rich, jewel-like space if well lit.

ACCESSORIES

To authenticate the style, use oriental handles and hinges, or paint ordinary fittings in silver or glossy black. Bamboo steamers, woven stacking boxes, chopsticks and other natural pieces can be bought quite cheaply in oriental supermarkets. You don't have to adopt the scheme wholesale. Details in appropriate colours will tone with or complement the scheme.

FLOORS

Traditionally, woven tatami mats were used to divide the floorspace into a grid, sized to fit dividing screens, but these days woven sisal in a wicker pattern is an ideal alternative.

DETAILS

Lacquerware is readily available and reasonably priced: look for plates, coasters and bowls in glossy finishes.

Japanese Cabinet

ANY SMALL CUPBOARD CAN BE CONVERTED TO MAKE THIS DINING-ROOM CABINET. THE MAIN BODY OF THIS ONE HAS BEEN MADE USING MDF, WITH TWO SEMI-CIRCULAR PIECES OF MDF SUPERIMPOSED ON THE DOORS TO CREATE A DISTINCTIVELY JAPANESE SHAPE. THE GLOSSY LACQUER FINISH IS ACHIEVED WITH SEVERAL COATS OF VARNISH.

Materials and equipment
MDF cupboard • screwdriver • medium decorator's brush • emulsion paint in terracotta and black • acetate for stencil • glass sheet or cutting mat • masking tape • hot pen or craft knife • spray adhesive • stencil brush • gloss acrylic varnish • varnish brush • bradawl • screws • 4 cupboard rail-holders • length of bamboo of diameter to fit cupboard rail-holders • saw

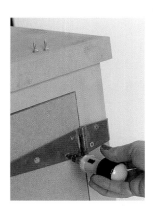

Step 1 Unscrew the hinges and any existing handles on the cupboard doors to facilitate painting.

Step 2 Paint the cupboard with two coats of terracotta emulsion and leave to dry.

Step 3 Photocopy and enlarge the single character stencil on page 131, and cut from acetate sheet. Lightly spray the back of the stencil with adhesive and centre it over the raised circle on the front of the cupboard. Using black emulsion and a stencil brush, stencil the image and leave to dry. The smaller character stencils on page 131 can be used to embellish the cupboard's edges and sides.

Step 4 Paint all surfaces of the cupboard with two coats of clear gloss varnish.

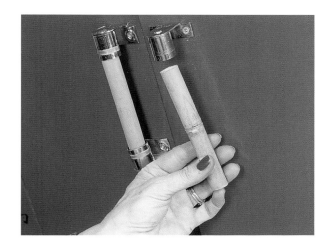

Step 5 Using a bradawl and screwdriver, fit two cupboard rail-holders to the cupboard doors to form the tops of the handles. Cut two 10cm/4in lengths of bamboo. Working with one handle at a time, slide a piece of bamboo into one of the rail-holders, then slot the other end into one of the two remaining rail-holders and screw it in place. Repeat to make the second handle.

Oriental Scroll

Step 1 Cut a piece of card to the desired size of the scroll, and mark the corners of the rectangle on the wall with a pencil.

Step 2 Lightly dip a paintbrush into terracotta emulsion, keeping the brush relatively dry. Using vertical strokes, brush the paint on to the wall to cover the marked area. Brush loosely, allowing some of the wall colour to show through. Leave to dry.

Step 3 Photocopy and enlarge the Japanese text on page 131, and cut a stencil from acetate. Spray the back of the stencil lightly with adhesive and position in the centre of the dry-brushed 'scroll'. Using a stencil brush sparsely loaded with black emulsion paint, stencil the characters individually.

A N INEXPENSIVE WAY TO EMULATE A TRADITIONAL SCROLL IS WITH A STENCIL OF JAPANESE CHARACTERS, APPLIED TO A LOOSELY PAINTED RECTANGLE OF TERRACOTTA EMULSION PAINT. THE WALLS ARE FIRST PAINTED IN A PARCHMENT COLOUR.

Step 4 Remove the stencil and reposition to complete the design. Leave to dry, then protect with a coat of clear matt acrylic varnish.

Materials and equipment
thin card • pencil and ruler • scissors • medium decorator's brush • emulsion paint in terracotta and black • photocopier • acetate for stencil • glass sheet or cutting mat • masking tape • hot pen or craft knife • spray adhesive • stencil brush • matt acrylic varnish' • varnish brush

Sliding Screen

S LIDING SCREENS, ORIGINALLY MADE OF COMPRESSED RICE STRAW, ARE AN ESSENTIAL INGREDIENT OF JAPANESE STYLE. THEY ARE EASY TO RE-CREATE AT HOME USING PAINTED GARDEN TRELLIS BACKED WITH TRACING PAPER. HUNG FROM A WOODEN POLE, PAINTED BLACK AND CONNECTED BY COAT-HANGER HOOKS, THIS SCREEN SLIDES IN FRONT OF A PAIR OF FRENCH DOORS DURING THE DAY, FILTERING A SOFT TRANSLUCENT LIGHT.

Materials and equipment

garden trellis to fit window • black emulsion paint • medium decorator's paintbrush • wooden curtain pole, twice the width of window • electric drill • 2 coat-hanger hooks • tracing paper • staple gun and staples • craft knife or wallpaper trimming knife

Step 1 Paint the trellis with black emulsion paint on one side only. Paint the curtain pole and fittings to match. Leave to dry.

Step 2 Using an electric drill with a fine bit, drill a hole in the top edge of the trellis at the first strut in from each end.

Step 3 Screw a coat-hanger hook into each hole.

Step 4 Staple sheets of tracing paper to the reverse side of the trellis, making joins where necessary. Trim away any joins which overlap to make sure they are not visible from the front.

Step 5 Hang the screen in place by hooking the coat-hanger hooks over the pole.

Bamboo Plant Support

Step 2 Push the two longest pieces of bamboo into the soil behind the orchids. Using re-usable putty adhesive to secure them temporarily, connect the shortest lengths of bamboo to the two uprights to form a diagonal cross.

Step 3 Using four strands of raffia together, tie the bamboo canes at each joint. Cut the raffia leaving the short ends to form tufts.

Step 4 Position the two 30cm/12in lengths of bamboo horizontally across the uprights, about one-third and two-thirds of the way up, and tie as before.

M OST ORCHIDS ARE SOLD ATTACHED TO A THIN WOODEN SUPPORT. THIS SIMPLE BAMBOO TRELLIS IS A DECORATIVE WAY TO SECURE TWO ORCHIDS IN A WICKER TROUGH.

Materials and equipment
thin bamboo garden canes • ruler • secateurs or small saw • basket of orchids • re-usable putty adhesive • natural raffia • scissors

Step 1 Cut six pieces of bamboo: two should be approximately 45cm/18in, two approximately 30cm/12in and two 20cm/8in.

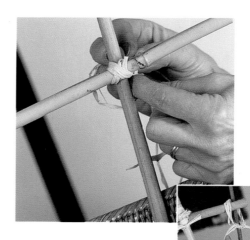

Step 5 Tie the stems to the support about 7–10cm/3–4in below the flower heads.

Stencils

關　然　皆　無　於
宮　昔　力　為　後
城　之　我　大　昆
之　池　尃　圜　此

Swedish
Hallway

THE SIMPLE ELEGANCE OF SWEDISH STYLE

COMBINES SOFT, TRADITIONAL LINES; UNCLUTTERED,

AIRY SPACES; PLENTY OF CREAMY-WHITE, PAINTED

WOODWORK AND MUTED, FADED COLOURS. THE

LOOK IS EXTREMELY EASY TO LIVE WITH AND APPEALS

TO MODERNISTS WITH A TRADITIONAL STREAK AS

WELL AS CITY-DWELLERS WITH NOSTALGIC

LONGINGS FOR A RURAL ENVIRONMENT. ABOVE ALL,

IT IS COUNTRIFIED AND UNCOMPLICATED, WITH ITS

RESTRAINED DECORATIVE CONTENT RESULTING IN

A SIMPLE, ROMANTIC ATMOSPHERE.

Focus on Style

Swedish Gustavian style derived its name from the reigns of Gustav III and IV of Sweden (1770–1809), and in essence it was a less ornate rendering of the French Empire and rococo style. Later, rustic Swedish style was popularized through the paintings and writings of the late 19th-century artist, Carl Larsson, depicting interiors that were a blend of traditional designs with fresh, clear colour, light and surface pattern. This style became recognized as quintessentially Swedish and has been widely marketed in furniture shops the world over.

Most Swedish colours are strongly influenced by that famously clear, northern light, and although it can never be reproduced exactly, a muslin or voile blind, or curtains that filter a white light, certainly help to accentuate the special Swedish look.

Texture plays an important part, as many old Swedish interiors were panelled. Fake panels can be created using moulding or tongue-and-groove boarding, painted to match the walls. Although floor-to-ceiling panelling is typical, it is easier and less expensive to board up to dado height only. Above this, panel shapes can be created either by painting different thicknesses of parallel lines or using a delicate border stencil. White, painted floorboards, limed beech or oak, or bleached, natural wooden boards were typical, but a simulated wooden floor can take their place.

WALLS

The Swedish palette is mostly pale, soft but clear, muted but not muddy. Pale, warm grey is a popular wall colour, punctuated with muted tones of green, yellow ochre, denim blue and terracotta. Deeper paint colours work well on tongue-and-groove boarding or for picking out alcoves, windowsills and surrounds. Keep to solid matt, rather than shiny textures. Chalky paints can be protected with a matt acrylic varnish.

FABRICS
Plain muslins, voiles and embroidered fabrics are most popular; checks and stripes are also typical. Patterns on textiles tend to be in a single colour on a cream background, and designs are usually of tightly ordered ribbons and flowers. Lace gives a more traditional Swedish look.

DETAILS
With short summers, Scandinavian accents include reminders of summer wherever possible. Flowers are most evocative of the season, hence a garland of flowers around a candlestick and a dried flower head to decorate a table napkin. In old Swedish country houses, picture frames and panel mouldings were gilded and given antiqued edges.

ACCESSORIES
Simple brass ring handles for painted chests are typical of the style. For an off-white kitchen, blue and white china is an alternative to plain white knobs. Otherwise, simply paint ordinary wooden handles in a Swedish colour to match the furniture.

FURNITURE
A good range of Swedish reproduction furniture is available to buy, but to save money you could find a junk piece and paint it in a typical Swedish colour: earthy red, muted green, grey or off-white. There is a wealth of Swedish folk art to which you can refer for decorative inspiration. To achieve the faded quality characteristic of this style, apply a final coat of glaze tinted with raw umber.

Swedish Hallway **135**

Voile Swag and Tails

I N SWEDEN, IT HAS BEEN SAID THAT CURTAIN TREATMENTS ARE DESIGNED TO CONTROL LIGHT, NOT BLOCK IT OUT. OFF-WHITE VOILE, MUSLIN AND FINE COTTON ARE USED TO FILTER THAT CHARACTERISTIC, CLEAR NORTHERN LIGHT, EVEN ON GREY DAYS, AND A BLIND PROVIDES PRIVACY. IN THIS TREATMENT, AN INFORMAL SWAG OF VOILE OVER A GREY, GLAZED POLE FRAMES THE WINDOW WITH SOFT, ROMANTIC LINES.

Materials and equipment
piping cord • scissors • white curtain voile • drawing pins • dressmakers' pins • sewing machine and matching thread

Step 1 Hang a length of piping cord over your curtain pole to create the desired shape of swag and length of tails. Cut the cord to that length and use it as a guide to cut a length of voile.

Step 2 Drape the voile over the pole, fixing it temporarily with drawing pins. Make sure that the tails are equal and the swag is centred. Mark the two inside top points of the swag with dressmakers' pins.

Step 3 Remove the voile from the pole. At each pin mark, fold the fabric and pin a dart about 20cm/8in deep spanning half the width of the fabric.

Step 4 Tear off the selvage of some leftover voile to use as tape stays. Cut the strip into eight 25cm/10in lengths and fold each one in half. At the folded ends, pin four ties at equal intervals into the two lines of pinned darts, then machine stitch the darts.

Step 5 Cut both ends of the voile swag at a gentle angle of about 25 degrees, so that they slope down towards the window. Machine hem all raw edges. Arrange the voile to create an even swag, and hold in place by tying each tape to the curtain pole.

Panelling with Stencils

Step 1 Photocopy and if necessary enlarge the leaf border stencil, on page 141, and cut it out of a sheet of acetate. Calculate the precise size and positioning of the panels for your room; then, using a plumb line and a long piece of straight moulding, mark with a pencil the outer edge of the two vertical stencils. Complete the panel outline by drawing in the two horizontal edges.

Step 2 Fold a square of card to make a right-angled triangle for use as a mitring template. Spray the back of the stencil lightly with adhesive and position it on the wall in one corner of the first panel. Place the triangular card over the end of the stencil and, using it as a guide, butt a strip of masking tape against it at the same 45 degree angle.

Wall decoration in the Gustavian period was discreet, often featuring painted stripes, and for bedrooms floral festoons were much favoured. Another decorative effect was the application of stencilled borders to plain or subtly colourwashed walls. The leaf stencil used here is an easy way to recreate the panelled look.

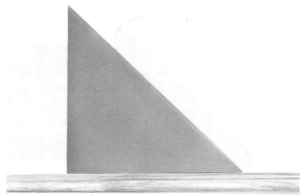

Step 3 Using a stencil brush, stencil the design in denim blue paint, then shade with gilt cream. Reposition the stencil to complete the panel, mitring the corners as before. Leave to dry for 24 hours, as the gilt cream is oil-based.

Materials and equipment

photocopier • acetate for stencil • glass sheet or cutting mat • masking tape • hot pen or craft knife • plumb line • length of straight moulding • pencil • thin card • spray adhesive • stencil brush • emulsion paint in denim blue • gilt cream

Chest of Drawers

Step 1 Sand down the chest and paint in two coats of pale grey emulsion, leaving to dry between coats.

Step 2 Mix a glaze by combining a teaspoonful of raw umber artist's acrylic paint with a cupful of acrylic scumble glaze. Apply with an ordinary brush in a horizontal direction and then drag with a dry dragging brush. Leave to dry.

A N OFF-WHITE BASE COAT, FINISHED WITH A COAT OF DRAGGED, RAW UMBER GLAZE IS THE FORMAT USED BY MOST SWEDISH-STYLE FURNITURE MANUFACTURERS TO CREATE THE FADED ANTIQUE LOOK. THE STENCIL IN DENIM BLUE AND OLD GOLD IS TYPICAL OF THE RESTRAINED DECORATION INSPIRED BY FRENCH ROCOCO AND PARED DOWN TO SUIT SWEDISH TASTE. SOME ALTERNATIVE SWEDISH-STYLE COLOURWAYS WOULD BE AN OCHRE BASE WITH BLUE-GREY DECORATION; A GREY-GREEN BASE STENCILLED IN OFF-WHITE WITH GREEN SHADING; OR A DOVE-GREY BASE STENCILLED IN OFF-WHITE AND SHADED WITH BLUE CRAYON.

Step 3 Copy and enlarge the leaf stencil on page 141 and cut it out of a sheet of acetate. Spray the back of the stencil with adhesive and position in the centre of the middle drawer. Using a stencil brush, stipple in denim blue and when dry, apply highlights with gilt cream. Leave to dry for 24 hours, as the gilt cream is oil-based.

Step 4 Mask 2cm/¾in lines around the drawers (and the top of the chest, if you wish). Apply white paint faintly with a stencil brush to produce a cloudy effect (it should not be too dense). Lift off the masking tape and when dry, protect the whole chest with a coat of acrylic varnish.

Materials and equipment

chest of drawers • sandpaper • emulsion paint in pale grey, denim blue and white • decorator's paintbrush • artist's acrylic paint in raw umber • acrylic scumble glaze • paint kettle • dragging brush • photocopier • acetate for stencil • glass sheet or cutting mat • masking tape • hot pen or craft knife • spray adhesive • stencil brush • gilt cream • matt acrylic varnish • varnish brush

Painted Pots

A ROW OF TRAILING PELARGONIUMS IN TERRACOTTA POTS SET ON A WIDE WINDOW LEDGE IS TYPICAL OF THE SWEDISH STYLE. THE POTS ARE PAINTED ALTERNATELY IN TWO TONES OF GREY PAINT.

Materials and equipment

terracotta flowerpots • emulsion in pale grey, mid-grey and white • decorator's paintbrush • chopstick • matt acrylic varnish • varnish brush

Step 1 Using different shades of grey emulsion for alternate pots, paint each pot with two coats and leave to dry.

Step 2 Dip the base of a chopstick in white emulsion and stamp the pots with equally spaced round blobs. Leave to dry, then apply two coats of acrylic varnish.

Stencils

Suppliers

NEW ENGLAND BATHROOM (pages 12–21) Walls, Antique Cladding, B & Q, painted in Aegean Blue and Regency White emulsion, Paint Magic. Natural Beech floor, Pergo. Towels, Christy. Pluto washbasin, Vitra. Shelves, Jali. Shutters, The Shutter Shop. Accessories, The Pier and Fieldhouse. Shells, Shell World. Rope handles, Turnstyle Designs.

COUNTRY BREAKFAST ROOM (pages 22–31) Walls, Rosie wallpaper, Cath Kidston. Reeded panelling and floorboards, B & Q. Floor stencils CL02 and CL06, The Cutting Light. Curtains, Felbrigg in pink, Bennison Fabrics. Cushions and tablecloth, Cath Kidston. Display shelf: style WC5, by Scumble Goosie, painted in Verdigris emulsion, Fired Earth. Ivan gateleg table, Cargo Homeshop, painted in Regency White emulsion, Paint Magic, and crackle glaze, Polyvine. Lamp, Laura Ashley. Chairs, Ann May. Pine shelves, Homebase. Hand-painted pottery, Rachel Miles.

MEXICAN DINING ROOM (pages 32–43) Walls, Bengal Rose 2000 emulsion, with border in Mint 1057, Blue Violet 1097 and Silver 1060, all Bristol UK. Rush-seated chairs, Ikea, painted in Chrome Yellow 1049, Mint 1057 and Orange 1042, all Bristol UK. Chest, shutters and dresser base no 9132, Jali, painted in Night Time emulsion, Homebase Studio range. Bowls made from Art Mâché by Specialist Crafts. Floor: seagrass, Original Seagrass Company. Silver plates and bowls, Culinary Concepts. Glasses and large terracotta pot, The Pier. Silks, Trade Eighty.

MODERN LIVING ROOM (pages 44–53) Walls, Sea Green emulsion, Farrow & Ball for Designers Guild. Floor, Pergo. Coffee table, Purves & Purves. Artist's canvas, Winsor & Newton. Fairy lights, Habitat. Cube footstools and Big Bean chair, Designers Guild. Star-shaped handles, Knobs & Knockers. Test tubes, John Bell & Croydon. Glass knobs, Bombay Duck. Chrome knobs, Glover & Smith.

EARLY AMERICAN BEDROOM (pages 54–63) Walls, Antique Cladding, B&Q. Bed and bedside tables, Laura Ashley. Bedlinen and accessories, Shaker Shop. Stencils, The Cutting Light. Floor, Pergo. Voile organza curtains, The Blue Door. Bialitt wardrobe, Ikea.

SUMMER GARDEN ROOM (pages 64–73) Walls, Apple Green emulsion, Laura Ashley. White floor tiles, World's End Tiles. Bench, planter, glasses and glazed pots, The Blue Door. Trellis and chairs, The Chelsea Gardener. Green and cream voile, Malabar Cotton Co. Glass knobs, Bombay Duck. Table: ceramic paints and pens, Pebeo.

TUSCAN HALLWAY (pages 74–85) Walls, Suffolk Pink emulsion with Spanish Terracotta colourwash; mosaic border stencil No

CL11, The Cutting Light, painted in Sundried Tomato, Yellow Sahara and Swedish Green, all by Paint Works. Floor, Sand emulsion; mosaic tile stencil painted in Pumice and Swedish Green, all by Paintworks. Curtain swag, Nabob Silk, JAB International. Console table, style FT4 Demi Lune, Scumble Goosie, with metal leaf, Staedtler. Chair, candle stand and pots, Elephant.

VICTORIAN BATHROOM (pages 86–97) Walls, yellow and white fabric, Baer & Ingram; panelling, Wickes, painted in China Blue emulsion, Fired Earth. Floor, Amtico. Window, Glass Etch Spray, Humbrol; self-adhesive lead tape, Peels of London; self-adhesive vinyl, X-Film UK. Curtains, Script, Hill & Knowles. Cupboard, style TV1, Scumble Goosie. Towels, Christy. Adelphi washbasin, Bathroom Discount Store. Armchair and wall-lights, Laura Ashley. Silk, Blue 985, Trade Eighty. Gilt cream, Liberon. Frames, Josie Bostock. Stencils, The Cutting Light.

ROMANTIC PARISIAN BEDROOM (pages 98–109) Walls, Rodeo Drive emulsion, Crown; stencils, The Cutting Light. Carpet: Sandstone 2010, Stoddard. Bed, bedside tables and bedlinen, Damask. Silk for canopy, Trade Eighty. Curtains, Vizaya Pearl and Embroidered Organza, Chase Erwin; Galatea Mimas lilac voile, Osborne & Little; poles, Artisan; clips, Cope & Timmins. Stool, Dormy House, upholstered in F 9191/02 Giradeau Paul Violet, Designers Guild. Console table, Dormy House. Vases, Designers Guild. Mirror mosaic, D. W. & G. Heath. Gilt cream, Liberon.

FRENCH RURAL KITCHEN (pages 110–121) Walls, Duck Egg Blue emulsion, Paint Magic. Floor, Amboise No 504098 flagstones, World's End Tiles. Armoire, style WD2, Scumble Goosie, painted in Impasto textured paint with top coats of Toffee Fudge and Saffron, both Paint Magic; stencil, The Cutting Light; handles, Knobs & Knockers. Butcher's block and chairs, Chalon. Pottery plates and saucepans, Divertimenti. Wicker vegetable rack and wire baskets, Summerill & Bishop. Plates painted by Onella at Brush and Bisque-It.

JAPANESE DINING ROOM (pages 122–131) Walls, Limestone emulsion, Paintworks. Seagrass on floor, Original Seagrass Company. Trellis for screen, Homebase. Oriental commode, Blankers, painted in Chinese Red, Paint Magic. Calligraphy stencils, The Cutting Light. Chairs, The Pier. Tableware and other accessories, Neal Street East. Handles shown on page 125, Clayton-Munroe.

SWEDISH HALLWAY (pages 132–141) Walls, Regency White emulsion, Paint Magic; stencils, The Cutting Light. Beech floor, Pergo. Curtain voile, Price & Co. Chest of drawers, style 3D3, Scumble Goosie, painted in Regency White emulsion with scumble glaze, Polyvine, and artist's acrylics, Winsor & Newton; handles, Relics. Chair and accessories, Nordic Style.

Acknowledgements

SO MANY PEOPLE HELPED ME WITH THIS BOOK, BUT MY MOST IMPORTANT LIFELINE WAS PRAYER. SO MY INEXPRESSIBLE FIRST THANK YOU HAS TO BE TO MY HEAVENLY FATHER WHO IN JESUS' NAME ALWAYS ANSWERED ALL MY REQUESTS FOR INSPIRATION AND HELP, MAKING THE PRODUCTION OF THIS BOOK FREE OF WORRY AND VERY GREAT FUN.

I AM SO GRATEFUL TO ALI MYER AND LINDSAY PORTER, AND ALL THE TALENTED TEAM AT DAVID & CHARLES WHO GAVE ME VALUABLE FEEDBACK AND SO MUCH ENCOURAGEMENT. I AM SO GRATEFUL TOO TO JON BOUCHIER, THE PHOTOGRAPHER, WHO NOT ONLY TOOK THE MOST BEAUTIFUL PHOTOGRAPHS BUT OFTEN GAVE ME HANDS-ON HELP WITH SAW AND HAMMER. SALEENA KHARA HELPED ME DECORATE MANY OF THE ROOM SETS AND DESIGN THE STENCILS, MOST OF THEM ESPECIALLY PRODUCED FOR THIS BOOK BY THE CUTTING LIGHT.

FINALLY I WOULD LIKE TO THANK THE COMPANIES WHO GENEROUSLY SUPPLIED MATERIALS AND LOANED PRODUCTS TO MAKE THE BOOK POSSIBLE. THEIR ADDRESSES AND DETAILS OF THE PRODUCTS ARE LISTED ABOVE AND OPPOSITE.

Addresses

Amtico, Kingfield Road, Coventry CV6 5AA (02476) 861400

Ann May, 80 Wandsworth Bridge Road, London SW6 (020) 7731 0862

Artisan Curtain Rails, Bushell Street Mills, Bushell Street, Preston PR1 2SP (01772) 203 444

B & Q plc, Shakespeare Road, Eastleigh, Hampshire SO50 4SF (023) 8025 6256

Baer & Ingram, 273 Wandsworth Bridge Road, London SW6 2TX (020) 7736 6111

Bathroom Discount Centre, 297 Munster Road, London SW6 6BW (020) 7381 4222

Bennison Fabrics, 16 Holbein Place, London SW1W 8NL (020) 7730 8076

Blankers, Unit 4, Durham Way, Heath Park, Honiton EX14 8SQ (0140) 447730

The Blue Door, 74 Church Road, London SW13 9HH (020) 8748 9785

Bombay Duck, 231 The Vale, Acton, London W3 7QS (020) 8749 8001

Bristol UK Ltd, 12 The Arches, Maygrove Road, London NW6 2DS (020) 7624 0686

The Brush 'n' Bisque-It, 77 Church Road, London SW13 9HH (020) 8563 1515

Cargo Homeshop, Whiteleys, 133 Queensway, London W2 4YL (020) 7229 4449

Cath Kidston, 8 Clarendon Cross, London W11 4AP (020) 7221 4000

Chalon UK, Hambridge Mill, Hambridge, Somerset TA10 0BP (01458) 254600

Chase Erwin Ltd, 22 Chelsea Harbour Design Centre, London SW10 0XE (020) 7352 7271

The Chelsea Gardener, 125 Sydney Street, London SW3 6NR (020) 7352 5656

Christy Towels, PO Box 19, Newton Street, Hyde, Cheshire SK14 4NP (0161) 368 1961

Clayton-Munroe Ltd, 2 Kingston Workshops, Staverton, Totnes, Devon TQ9 6AR (01803) 762626

Cope & Timmins Ltd, Angel Road Works, Advent Way, Edmonton, London N18 3AY (020) 8803 6481

Crofts & Assinder Ltd, 79 Lombard Street, Birmingham B12 0QX (0121) 622 1074

Crown Berger Ltd, Crown House, Hollins Road, Darwen, Lancashire BB3 0BJ (01254) 704951

Culinary Concepts, 51 Searles Road, The Paragon, London SE1 4YL (020) 7277 0088

Cutting Light, Wroxton Cottage, Lower Road, Chorleywood, Hertfordshire WD3 5LA 01923 284860

Damask, 3/4 Broxholme House, New Kings Road, London SW6 4AA (020) 7731 3553

Designers Guild, 267 and 277 Kings Road, London SW3 5EN (020) 7351 5775

Divertimenti Ltd, 139 Fulham Road, SW3 6SD (020) 7581 8065

Dormy House, Stirling Park, East Portway Industrial Estate, Andover, Hampshire SP10 3TZ (01264) 365808

Elephant Ltd, 167 Queensway, London W2 4SB (020) 7467 0630

Farrow & Ball, Unit 33, Uddens Industrial Estate, Wimborne, Dorset BH21 7NL (01202) 876141

Fieldhouse, 89 Wandsworth Bridge Road, London SW6 2TD (020) 7736 7547

Fired Earth Tiles plc, Twyford Mill, Oxford Road, Adderbury, Oxfordshire OX17 3SX (01295) 814399

Glover & Smith, 9a Winchester Street, Overton, Nr Basingstoke, Hampshire RG25 3NP (01256) 773012

Habitat UK Ltd, 196 Tottenham Court Road, London W1P 9LD (020) 7255 2545

D.W. & G. Heath (Croydon) Ltd, 19 Portley Wood Road, Whyteleafe, Surrey CR3 0BQ (020) 8657 6349

Hill & Knowles, Chelsea Harbour Design Centre, London SW10 0XE (020) 7376 4686

Homebase Ltd, Beddington House, Railway Approach, Wallington, Surrey SM6 0DX (020) 8784 7200

Humbrol Ltd, Marfleet, Hull HU9 5NE (01482) 701191

Ikea Ltd, 2 Drury Way, London NW10 0TH (020) 8208 5600

Integra Products, Eastern Avenue, Lichfield, Staffordshire WS13 7SB (01543) 267100

JAB International Furnishings Ltd, 1–15 Chelsea Harbour Design Centre, London SW10 0XE (020) 7349 9323

Jali Ltd, Apsley House, Chartham, Canterbury, Kent CT4 7PT (01227) 831710

Knobs & Knockers, 567 Kings Road, London SW6 2EB (020) 7384 2884

Laura Ashley, 27 Bagley's Lane, London SW6 2QA (020) 7880 5100

Liberon Waxes, Mountfield Industrial Estate, Learoyd Road, New Romney, Kent TN28 8XU (01797) 367555

The Malabar Cotton Co Ltd, 31–33 Southbank Business Centre, Ponton Road, SW8 5BL (020) 7501 4200

Rachel Miles, 8 Victoria Terrace, Cheltenham, Gloucestershire GL52 6BN (01242) 23001

Neal Street East, 5 Neal Street, London WC2H 9PU (020) 7240 0135

Nordic Style, 109 Lots Road, London SW10 0RN (020) 7351 1755

Original Seagrass Co, Shrewsbury Road, Craven Arms, Shropshire SY7 9NW (01588) 673666

Osborne & Little plc, 49 Temperley Road, London SW12 8QE (020) 8675 2255

Paint Magic, 48 Golborne Road, London W10 5SU (020) 8960 9960

Paintworks, 5 Elgin Crescent, London W11 2JA (020) 7792 8012

Pebeo UK, 416 Solent Business Centre, Millbrook Road West, Millbrook, Southampton SO15 0HW (023) 8090 1914

Peels of London, PO Box 160, Richmond TW10 7XL (020) 8948 0689

Pergo Ltd, 18–20 Cromwell Business Park, Chipping Norton, Oxfordshire OX7 5SR (01608) 646200

The Pier Ltd, 91 Kings Road, London SW3 4PA (020) 7351 7100

Plasti-Kote Ltd, PO Box 867, Pampisford, Cambridge CB2 4XP (01223) 836400

Polyvine Ltd, Vine House, Rockhampton, Berkeley, Gloucestershire GL13 9DT (01454) 261276

Price & Co, Regency House, North Street, Portslade, East Sussex BN41 1DH (01273) 421999

Purves & Purves, 80/81 & 83 Tottenham Court Road, London W1P 9HD, 0207 580 8223

Relics, 35 Bridge Street, Witney, Oxfordshire OX8 6DA (01993) 704611

Scumble Goosie, Lewiston Mill, Toadsmoor Road, Brimscombe, Stroud, Gloucestershire GL5 2TB (01453) 731305

The Shaker Shop, 27 Harcourt Street, London W1H 1DT (020) 7724 5986

Shell World, 41 Kings Road, Brighton BN1 1NA (01273) 327664

The Shutter Shop, Taplins Farm, Church Lane, Hartley Wintney, Hampshire RG27 8NX (01252) 844575

Specialist Crafts, PO Box 247, Leicester LE1 9QS (0116) 251 0405

Staedtler UK Ltd, Pontyclun, Mid Glamorgan CF72 8YJ (01443) 237421

Stoddard Carpets Ltd, Glenpatrick Road, Elderslie, Johnstone, Renfrewshire PA5 9UA (01505) 577000

Summerill & Bishop Ltd, 100 Portland Road, London W11 4LQ (020) 7221 4566

Trade Eighty, 63 Riding House Street, London W1P 7PP (020) 7637 5188

Turnstyle Designs, Village Street, Bishops Tawton, Barnstaple, Devon EX32 0DG (01271) 325325

Vitra, 121 Milton Park, Abingdon, Oxfordshire OX14 4SA (01235) 820400

Wickes Ltd, 120–128 Station Road, Harrow, Middlesex HA1 2QB (020) 8901 2000

Winsor & Newton, Whitefriars Avenue, Wealdstone, Harrow, Middlesex HA3 5RH (020) 8424 3200

World's End Tiles Ltd, Railway Goods Yard, Silverthorne Road, London SW8 3HE (020) 7819 2100

X-Film UK, PO Box 37, Unit 3, Dalroad Enterprises Estate, Luton LU1 1YW (01582) 453308

Suppliers of equipment

Fiskars Ltd, Newlands Avenue, Bridgend, Mid Glamorgan CF31 2XA (01656) 655595 (scissors)

L. G. Harris & Co Ltd, PO Vox 2844, Stoke Prior, Bromsgrove, Worcestershire B60 4DE (01527) 575441 (paintbrushes)

3M UK plc, 3M House, PO Box 1, Bracknell, Berkshire RG12 1JU (0990) 360036 (masking tape)

Index